"Steven Spielberg's *Lincoln* is a work (instantly invite repeat viewings . . . Kushner's sc1ip˪ ᴜ .... than just elegant in its compression and exposition. It is steeped in the traditions of a political dramaturgy that were familiar to Shakespeare and Schiller but that have not often been practiced in American historical films."

—GEOFFREY O'BRIEN, NEW YORK REVIEW OF BOOKS

"Spielberg and Kushner marched straight down the center of national memory, the moment of glory and anguish, and they got it right . . . Kushner realized that nineteenth century politics were essentially theatrical. He elevated the back-and-forth interplay of meetings and debate into eloquence, tirade, insult, rodomontade . . . in Kushner's version, the range of speech is almost Shakespearean." —DAVID DENBY, NEW YORKER

"It's a hell of a thing, this Lincoln . . . all forward thrust and hot-damn urgency. Screenwriter Tony Kushner blows the dust off history by investing it with flesh, blood, and churning purpose."

—PETER TRAVERS, ROLLING STONE

"A lyrical, ingeniously structured screenplay. Lincoln is one of the most authentic biographical dramas I've ever seen . . . grand and immersive. It plugs us into the final months of Lincoln's presidency with a purity that makes us feel transported as if by time machine."

—OWEN GLEIBERMAN, ENTERTAINMENT WEEKLY

"Catnip for political junkies, *Lincoln* might be called "Our Better Angels in America." What more auspicious time to release a film about the president who served during the Civil War than these insecure, battle-weary times of ours? "

—JAMES VERNIERE, BOSTON HERALD

"Better than any other, the movie captures President Lincoln's awkward, shuffling, distinctly democratic greatness. The low in him that caused sophisticates to sneer. The high in him shaped by Shakespeare and Euclid. The humanity, frailty and aching introspection. The shrewdness, decisiveness and ferocious will. It is the democratic faith that exceptional leaders can be found among common folk."

—MICHAEL GERSON, WASHINGTON POST

LINCOLN

OTHER BOOKS BY TONY KUSHNER
PUBLISHED BY THEATRE COMMUNICATIONS GROUP

Angels in America: A Gay Fantasia on National Themes
Part One: Millennium Approaches
Part Two: Perestroika

A Bright Room Called Day

Caroline, or Change

Death & Taxes: Hydriotaphia & Other Plays

A Dybbuk and Other Tales of the Supernatural

Homebody/Kabul

The Illusion
(adapted from Pierre Corneille)

*Thinking about the Longstanding Problems of Virtue
and Happiness: Essays, a Play, Two Poems and a Prayer*

A FILM BY STEVEN SPIELBERG

LINCOLN

THE SCREENPLAY

TONY KUSHNER

Foreword by Doris Kearns Goodwin

THEATRE COMMUNICATIONS GROUP
NEW YORK
2012

Lincoln is published by Theatre Communications Group, Inc., 520 Eighth Avenue, 24th Floor, New York, NY 10018-4156

The publication of *Lincoln* by Tony Kushner is made possible in part by the New York State Council on the Arts with the support of Governor Andrew Cuomo and the New York State Legislature.

TCG books are exclusively distributed to the book trade by Consortium Book Sales and Distribution.

Cataloging-in-Publication Data is on file at the Library of Congress, Washington, D.C.

ISBN: 978-1-55936-453-9 (pbk.)
ISBN: 978-1-55936-454-6 (hardcover)
ISBN: 978-1-55936-767-7 (ebook)

CONTENTS

FOREWORD

By Doris Kearns Goodwin

I first met Tony Kushner on April 25, 2006. Five years earlier, Steven Spielberg had acquired the rights to my then unfinished book: *Team of Rivals: The Political Genius of Abraham Lincoln*. From the start, Steven knew that he wanted to make a film centered on Lincoln the man, rather than the battles of the Civil War. And he wanted Tony to write the script.

Tony was hesitant. "The subject and the man just seemed too big," he said. To help Tony's process of decision, Steven asked me to arrange a daylong meeting with a dozen or so of my fellow historians. "You can ask them questions and all of your doubts will be answered," Steven assured Tony.

For seven hours, with Steven directing a wide-ranging conversation, we talked about Lincoln, sharing stories about his temperament, his laborious efforts to educate himself, his string of political failures, the timber of his voice, the way he walked. We argued about the depth of his depression, the nature of his marriage, and his relationship with his children. We had differing opinions about Mary Todd Lincoln, his generals and the members of his cabinet. I remember looking over at Tony on several occasions, worrying that through our animated discussion, we were simply confirming that the story of Abraham Lincoln was, indeed, too big, too complex to capture in a movie.

At the end of the meeting, Tony came over to me, still full of doubts. "I know exactly what you're feeling," I said. "When I started *Team of Rivals* ten years ago, I had similar fears. With fifteen thousand books already published about the president and the Civil War, I knew I had to find my own angle. Then, even when I found my focus, by centering the story on Lincoln's leadership skills, on the way he handled the troubled relationships with his former rivals, I still worried. And so will you. But I can promise you one thing. You'll never regret any time you spend with Abraham Lincoln." I then confessed that having finished the book, I missed waking up with Lincoln every morning, thinking about him every night when I went to bed. I told him what Ida Tarbell, the journalist/historian had said at the turn of the twentieth century when asked to explain why so many people spent so many years writing about Lincoln. It is simple, she said, it is because he is so companionable. Tony later told me that our talk that afternoon played an important role in his decision to accept the challenge.

No writer was better suited for the task. One of the most celebrated playwrights of our time, Tony Kushner is passionate about politics and language, the twin pillars of Lincoln's life. The nineteenth century was an age when the command of the spoken word was central to political success, when thousands of people stood riveted for three or four hours while political opponents debated in the open air, when audiences felt free to interject comments, cheer for their champion, bemoan the jabs of his opponent. It was an age when politics generated the enthusiasm and devotion we now devote to sports. In these pages, Tony perfectly captures this raucous era.

The screenplay took six years to write. At one point it was five hundred pages long, covering the last four months of Lincoln's presidency. I saw perhaps a half dozen different drafts, each one compressing the time frame more and more, until the brilliant decision was made to focus on the single month of January 1865, to make the congressional fight for the Thirteenth Amendment outlawing slavery the core of the film—a thriller of a story that has a beginning, middle and end.

The magic of the screenplay, however, goes far beyond the dramatic plot; Tony's lasting triumph is the compelling portrait he paints of Abraham Lincoln—revealing his fierce ambition, astonishing political skills, willingness to take responsibility for unbearable choices, melancholy temperament, gift for storytelling, life-affirming sense of humor, literary genius. Kushner's Lincoln comes so fully to life in these pages that you feel as if you are by his side, listening as he talks with his cabinet, greets petitioners, visits wounded soldiers in the hospital, wanders into the telegraph office, fights with his wife, comforts his son.

"I happen temporarily to occupy this big White House," Lincoln once told a group of soldiers. "I am a living witness that any one of your children may look to come here as my father's child has. It is in order that each of you have through this free government which we have enjoyed, an open field and a fair chance for your industry, enterprise and intelligence, that you may all have equal privileges in the race of life, with all its desirable aspirations. It is for this the struggle should be maintained."

In an age when we are cynical about politicians and frustrated with our political system, Tony Kushner's screenplay is a vivid testimony to the ultimate strength of our democratic form of government—the revolutionary idea, designed by our founding fathers and secured by the Civil War, that ordinary people can govern themselves without kings or queens, dictators or tsars. This noble experiment, Lincoln repeatedly said, is the "birthright" of our nation. It is up to each generation, as this majestic screenplay reminds us, to preserve that precious birthright.

December 2012

DORIS KEARNS GOODWIN is the Pulitzer Prize–winning author of many presidential histories, including *Team of Rivals: The Political Genius of Abraham Lincoln; No Ordinary Time: Franklin and Eleanor Roosevelt: The Home Front in World War II;* and *The Fitzgeralds and the Kennedys: An American Saga.*

CREDITS

Dreamworks Pictures, Twentieth Century Fox and
Reliance Entertainment present in association with
Participant Media
An Amblin Entertainment/Kennedy/
Marshall Company Production
A Steven Spielberg Film
Produced by Steven Spielberg and Kathleen Kennedy
Executive Producers Daniel Lupi, Jeff Skoll
and Jonathan King
Co-Producers Adam Somner and Kristie Macosko Krieger

Director: Steven Spielberg
Music: John Williams
Costume Design: Joanna Johnston
Editor: Michael Kahn, ACE
Production Design: Rick Carter
Director of Photography: Janusz Kaminski
Sound Design: Ben Burtt
Makeup Design: Lois Burwell
Writer's Assistant: Antonia Grilikhes-Lasky

Based in part on *Team of Rivals:*
The Political Genius of Abraham Lincoln
by Doris Kearns Goodwin

CAST OF CHARACTERS

THE LINCOLNS

President Abraham Lincoln	Daniel Day-Lewis
Mary Todd Lincoln	Sally Field
Tad Lincoln	Gulliver McGrath
Robert Lincoln	Joseph Gordon-Levitt

THE WHITE HOUSE STAFF

John Hay, Lincoln's assistant secretary	Joseph Cross
Elizabeth Keckley, Mrs. Lincoln's dressmaker	Gloria Reuben
John Nicolay, Lincoln's secretary	Jeremy Strong
Thomas Pendel, doorkeeper and Tad's bodyguard	Ford Flannagan
William Slade, Lincoln's valet	Stephen McKinley Henderson

THE CABINET

Secretary of State William H. Seward	David Strathairn
Secretary of War Edwin M. Stanton	Bruce McGill

Secretary of the Navy
   Gideon Welles   Grainger Hines
Attorney General James Speed   Richard Topol
Secretary of the Treasury
   William Fessenden   Walt Smith
Secretary of the Interior
   John Usher   Dakin Matthews
Postmaster General
   William Dennison   James Ike Eichling

THE REPUBLICANS

The Conservatives

Preston Blair   Hal Holbrook
Montgomery Blair   Byron Jennings
Elizabeth Blair Lee   Julie White
Representative Aaron
   Haddam, leader of the
   conservative Republicans   Gannon McHale

The Radicals

Representative Thaddeus Stevens   Tommy Lee Jones
Representative James M. Ashley   David Costabile
Representative Asa Vintner
   Litton   Stephen Spinella
Speaker of the House
   Schuyler Colfax   Bill Raymond
Senator Ben "Bluff" Wade   Wayne Duvall
Senator Charles Sumner   John Hutton

THE DEMOCRATS

House Minority Leader
   George H. Pendleton   Peter McRobbie
Representative Fernando Wood   Lee Pace
Representative
   George G. Yeaman   Michael Stuhlbarg
Representative
   Alexander H. Coffroth   Boris McGiver
Representative Clay Hawkins   Walton Goggins

Representative William Hutton — David Warshofsky
Representative Edwin LeClerk — John Moon
Representative Charles Hanson — Kevin Lawrence
          O'Donnell
Representative Nelson Merrick — Joseph Dellinger
Representative Homer Benson — Richard Warner
Representative Giles Stuart — Jamie Horton
Representative Jacob Graylor — Robert Peters
Representative Harold Hollister — Michael Ruff
Representative John Ellis — Ted Johnson

OTHER MEMBERS OF THE HOUSE OF REPRESENTATIVES

Clerk of the House
    Edward McPherson — Christopher Evan Welch
Sergeant-at-Arms — Alan Sader
Representative Hiram Price — Michael Stanton Kennedy
Representative
    Augustus Benjamin — Ken Lambert
Representative Arthur Bentleigh — Tom Belgrey
Representative Walter Appleton — Don Henderson Baker
Representative Josiah S.
    "Beanpole" Burton — Raynor Scheine
Representative Nehemiah Cleary — Armistead Nelson
          Wellford
Representative Walter H.
    Washburn — Todd Fletcher
Representative Meyer Straus — Charles Kinney
Representative Joseph Marstern — Joseph Carlson
Representative Chilton A. Elliot — Michael Goodwin
Representative Daniel G. Stuart — Edward McDonald
Representative
    Howard Guillefoyle — James Batchelder
Representative John F. McKenzie — Gregory Hosaflook
Representative Andrew E. Finck — Joe Kerkes
Representative John A. Kassim — William Kaffenberger
Representative Avon Hanready — Larry Van Hoose
Representative Rufus Warren — C. Brandon Marshall

SEWARD'S POLITICAL OPERATIVES

Richard Schell	Tim Blake Nelson
Robert Latham	John Hawkes
W. N. Bilbo	James Spader

THE CONFEDERATE PEACE COMMISSIONERS

Vice President of the Confederate States of America Alexander Stephens	Jackie Earle Haley
Former CSA Secretary of State Senator R. M. T. Hunter	Michael Shiflett
CSA Assistant Secretary of War Judge John A. Campbell	Gregory Itzin

THE WAR DEPARTMENT

Telegraph Operator David Homer Bates	Drew Sease
Telegraph Operator Samuel H. Beckwith	Adam Driver
Major Thomas Eckert	Robert Ruffin
Assistant Secretary of the Navy Gustavus V. Fox	John Lescault
Charles Benjamin, Stanton's chief clerk	Scott Wichmann

THE UNION ARMY

Lieutenant General Ulysses S. Grant	Jared Harris
Private Harold Green	Colman Domingo
Corporal Ira Clark	David Oyelowo
First White Soldier	Lukas Haas
Second White Soldier	Dane Dehaan
Lincoln's Bodyguard	Lancer Shull
Military Escort for the Peace Commissioners	Elijah Chester
Captain Nathan B. Saunders	Dave Hager
Lieutenant Colonel Ely S. Parker	Asa-Luke Twocrow

Sergeant at Grant's City Point Headquarters	Christopher Alan Stewart
Corporal at Grant's City Point Headquarters	Teddy Eck
Soldier One at the Capitol	Rich Wills
Soldier Outside the Capitol	Stephen Bozzo

IN THE MILITARY HOSPITAL

Doctor	George Turman
Wounded Soldiers:	Robert Wilharm, Kevin Kline, Sergeant John Jones, Paul Gowans, Joseph Miller

OTHER CHARACTERS

Mr. Jolly	Bill Camp
Mrs. Jolly	Elizabeth Marvel
Lydia Smith	S. Epatha Merkerson
Singer Performing Faust	John Bellemer
Singer Performing Marguerite .	Mary Dunleavy
Leonard Grover	Christopher Cartmill
Dr. Joseph K. Barnes	Robert Shepherd
Minerva, the Blairs' servant	Charmaine Crowell-White
Leo, the Blairs' servant	Ralph D. Edlow
White House Petitioner	Bob Ayers
Military Escort for the Peace Commissioners	Sean Haggerty
Confederate Officer	Stephen Dunn
The Philadelphia Abolitionist League:	Ambassador Jean Kennedy Smith, Shirley Augustine, Sarah Wylie, Margaret Ann McGowan, Hilary Montgomery
General Robert E. Lee	Christopher Boyer
Actor Playing Aladdin	Stephen Dunford
Actor Playing the Demon Afrit	David Doersch

LINCOLN

EXT. BATTLEFIELD, JENKINS' FERRY, ARKANSAS—DAY

Heavy gray skies hang over a flooded field, the water two
feet deep. Cannons and carts, half-submerged and tilted,
their wheels trapped in the mud below the surface, are still
yoked to dead and dying horses and oxen.

A terrible battle is taking place; two infantry companies,
Negro Union soldiers and white Confederate soldiers, knee-
deep in the water, staggering because of the mud beneath,
fight each other hand-to-hand, with rifles, bayonets, pistols,
knives and fists. There's no discipline or strategy, nothing
depersonalized: it's mayhem and each side intensely hates
the other. Both have resolved to take no prisoners.

>   HAROLD GREEN (V.O.)
>   Some of us was in the Second Kansas Col-
>   ored. We fought the rebs at Jenkins' Ferry
>   last April, just after they'd killed every
>   Negro soldier they captured at Poison
>   Springs.

EXT. PARADE GROUNDS ADJACENT TO THE
WASHINGTON NAVY YARD, ANACOSTIA RIVER—NIGHT

Rain and fog. Union Army companies are camped out
across the grounds. Preparations are being made for the
impending assault on the Confederate fortifications guard-
ing the port of Wilmington, North Carolina.

Two black soldiers stand before a bivouacked Negro unit:
HAROLD GREEN, an infantryman in his late thirties, and
IRA CLARK, a cavalryman in his early twenties. ABRAHAM
LINCOLN sits on a bench facing Harold and Ira; his stove-
pipe hat is at his side.

> **HAROLD GREEN**
> So at Jenkins' Ferry, we decided warn't taking
> no reb prisoners. And we didn't leave a one
> of 'em alive. The ones of us that didn't die
> that day, we joined up with the 116th U.S.
> Colored, sir. From Camp Nelson, Kentucky.

> **LINCOLN**
> What's your name, soldier?

> **HAROLD GREEN**
> Private Harold Green, sir.

> **IRA CLARK**
> I'm Corporal Ira Clark, sir. Fifth Massachu-
> setts Cavalry. We're waiting over there.

He nods in the direction of his cavalry.

> **IRA CLARK**
> We're leaving our horses behind, and ship-
> ping out with the 24th Infantry for the
> assault next week on Wilmington.

> **LINCOLN**
> (to Harold Green:)
> How long've you been a soldier?

HAROLD GREEN
Two year, sir.

LINCOLN
Second Kansas Colored Infantry, they
fought bravely at Jenkins' Ferry.

HAROLD GREEN
That's right, sir.

IRA CLARK
They killed a thousand rebel
soldiers, sir. They were very
brave.
(hesitating, then:)
And making three dollars less
each month than white soldiers.

Harold Green is a little startled at Clark's bluntness.

HAROLD GREEN
Us 2nd Kansas boys, whenever we fight now
we—

IRA CLARK
Another three dollars subtracted from our
pay for our uniforms.

HAROLD GREEN
That was true, yessir, but that changed—

IRA CLARK
Equal pay now. Still no commissioned
Negro officers.

LINCOLN
I am aware of it, Corporal Clark.

IRA CLARK
Yes, sir, that's good you're aware, sir. It's
only that—

HAROLD GREEN
(to Lincoln, trying to change the subject:)
You think the Wilmington attack is gonna be—

IRA CLARK
Now that white people have accustomed
themselves to seeing Negro men with guns,
fighting on their behalf, and now that they
can tolerate Negro soldiers getting the same
pay—in a few years perhaps they can abide
the idea of Negro lieutenants and captains.
In fifty years, maybe a Negro colonel. In a
hundred years—the vote.

Green's offended at the way Clark is talking to Lincoln.

LINCOLN
What'll you do after the war, Corporal
Clark?

IRA CLARK
Work, sir. Perhaps you'll hire me.

LINCOLN
Perhaps I will.

IRA CLARK
But you should know, sir, that I get sick at
the smell of bootblack and I can't cut hair.

Lincoln smiles.

LINCOLN
I've yet to find a man could cut mine so it'd
make any difference.

HAROLD GREEN
You got springy hair for a white man.

Lincoln laughs.

                    LINCOLN
          Yes, I do. My last barber hanged himself.
          And the one before that. Left me his scis-
          sors in his will.

Green laughs.

TWO WHITE SOLDIERS have come up, two young kids,
nervous and excited.

    FIRST WHITE SOLDIER   LINCOLN
President Lincoln, sir?   Evening, boys.

              SECOND WHITE SOLDIER
          Damn! Damn!
          We, we saw you, um. We were at, at—

              FIRST WHITE SOLDIER
          We was at Gettysburg!

    HAROLD GREEN   SECOND WHITE SOLDIER
You boys fight at Gettysburg?   DAMN I can't believe it's—

              FIRST WHITE SOLDIER
              (to Green, with mild contempt:)
          Naw, we didn't *fight* there.
          We just signed up last month.
          We saw him two years ago at the cemetery
          dedication.

              SECOND WHITE SOLDIER
          Yeah, we heard you speak! We . . . DAMN
          DAMN DAMN! Uh, hey, how tall are you
          anyway?!

              FIRST WHITE SOLDIER
          Jeez, SHUT up!

LINCOLN
Could you hear what I said?

FIRST WHITE SOLDIER
No, sir, not much, it was—

SECOND WHITE SOLDIER
(he recites, fast and mechanically:)
"Four score and seven years ago, our fathers
brought forth on this continent a new
nation, conceived in liberty and dedicated
to the proposition that all men are created
equal."

LINCOLN
That's good, thank you for—

FIRST WHITE SOLDIER
"Now we are engaged in a great civil war,
testing whether that nation or any nation
so conceived and so dedicated can long
endure. We are, we are, we are met on a
great battlefield of that war."

LINCOLN
Thank you, that's—

SECOND WHITE SOLDIER
"We have come to dedicate a portion of that
field as a final resting place for those who
here gave their lives that that nation might
live. It is . . ."
(He chokes up a little.)

FIRST WHITE SOLDIER
His uncles, they died on the second day of
fighting.

SECOND WHITE SOLDIER   A VOICE (O.C.)
I know the last part. "It is,   Company up! Move it out!
uh, it is rather—"

SOLDIERS all over the field rise up at the mustering of the
troops. Names of regiments, brigades, divisions are called:
all across the field, the men put out fires, put on knapsacks.

LINCOLN
(to the two white soldiers:)
You fellas best find your company.

FIRST WHITE SOLDIER
(saluting Lincoln:)
Thank you, sir. God bless you!

LINCOLN
God bless you.

The second white soldier salutes, and the two move out.

Green salutes Lincoln as well and glances at Clark, who
remains, looking down. Green leaves. Clark looks up, salutes
Lincoln and, turning smartly, walks toward his unit.

Then he stops, turns back, faces Lincoln, who watches him.
A beat, and then, in a tone of admiration and cautious
admonishment, reminding Lincoln of his promise:

IRA CLARK
"That we here highly resolve that these
dead shall not have died in vain—"

Clark salutes Lincoln again, turns again and walks away. Lincoln watches him go. As he walks into the fog, Clark continues reciting in a powerful voice:

IRA CLARK
"—That this nation, under God, shall have
a new birth of freedom—and that government of the people, by the people, for the
people, shall not perish from the earth."

Lincoln watches Clark until the fog's swallowed him up.

TITLE:
JANUARY, 1865
TWO MONTHS HAVE PASSED SINCE
ABRAHAM LINCOLN'S REELECTION
THE AMERICAN CIVIL WAR IS NOW IN ITS FOURTH YEAR

EXT. A SHIP AT SEA—NIGHT

A huge, dark, strange-looking steamship, part wood and
part iron, turreted like a giant ironclad monitor, is plowing
through the choppy black waters of an open sea.

Lincoln is alone, in darkness, on the deck, which has no
railing, open to the sea. The ship's tearing through rough
water, but there's little pitching, wind or spray. The deck is
dominated by the immense black gunnery turret.

LINCOLN (V.O.)
It's nighttime. The ship's moved by some
terrible power, at a terrific speed.

Lincoln stares out toward a barely discernible horizon, indi-
cated by a weird, flickering, leaden glow, which appears to
recede faster than the fast-approaching ship.

LINCOLN (V.O.)
Though it's imperceptible in the darkness,
I have an intuition that we're headed
towards a shore. No one else seems to be
aboard the vessel. I'm alone.

INT. MARY'S BOUDOIR, SECOND FLOOR OF THE
WHITE HOUSE—NIGHT

The room's cozy, attractive, cluttered, part dressmaker's
workshop, part repository of Mary's endless purchases: clothing, fabrics, knicknacks, carpets. Books everywhere.

Lincoln reclines on a French chair, too small for his lengthy
frame. He's in shirtsleeves, vest unbuttoned and tie unknot-
ted, shoeless. He has an open folio filled with documents on
his lap.

MARY LINCOLN sits opposite, in a nightgown, housecoat
and night cap. She watches him in her vanity mirror.

She looks frightened.

TITLE:
THE WHITE HOUSE

> LINCOLN
> I could be bounded in a nutshell and count
> myself a king of infinite space . . . were it
> not that I have bad dreams.
> I reckon it's the speed that's strange to me.
> I'm used to going a deliberate pace.

Mary looks at him, stricken with alarm.

> LINCOLN
> I should spare you. I shouldn't tell you my
> dreams.

> MARY
> I don't want to be spared if you aren't! And
> you spare me nothing.

He looks down at the carpet, then back up at her.

MARY

Perhaps perhaps it's the assault on Wilmington port. You dream about the ship before a battle, usually.

LINCOLN

(rapping lightly on his forehead:)
How's the coconut?

MARY

Beyond description.

She delicately touches her head.

MARY

Almost two years, nothing mends. Another casualty of the war. Who wants to listen to a useless woman grouse about her carriage accident?

LINCOLN

I do.

MARY

Stuff! You tell me dreams, that's all, I'm your soothsayer, that's all I am anymore, I'm not to be trusted with—even if it wasn't a carriage accident, even if it was an attempted assassination—

LINCOLN

It was most probably an—

MARY

It was an assassin. Whose intended target was you.

LINCOLN

How's the plans for the big shindy progressing?

MARY

I don't want to talk about parties! You don't
care about parties.

LINCOLN

Not much but they're a necessary—

MARY

(a revelation:)
I know . . . I know what it's about. The ship,
it isn't Wilmington port, it's not a military
campaign! It's the amendment to abolish
slavery! Why else would you force me to
invite demented radicals into my home?

Lincoln closes his folio.

MARY

You're going to try to get the amendment
passed in the House of Representatives, before
the term ends, before the inauguration.

LINCOLN

(standing:)
Don't spend too much money on the flub-
dubs.

Mary stands, goes up to him.

MARY

No one's loved as much as you, no one's
ever been loved so much, by the people,
you might do anything now. Don't, don't
waste that power on an amendment bill
that's sure of defeat.

Seeing that he's not going to discuss this, she turns away,
walking to an open window.

MARY

Did you remember Robert's coming home
for the reception?

Lincoln nods, though Mary isn't bothering to look at him.

MARY

I knew you'd forget.

She closes the window.

MARY

That's the ship you're sailing on. The Thirteenth Amendment. You needn't tell me
I'm right. I know I am.

She watches as he leaves the room, smiling in bitter victory:
she's right.

INT. HALLWAY, OUTSIDE MARY'S BOUDOIR—NIGHT

Lincoln encounters ELIZABETH KECKLEY, a light-skinned
black woman, thirty-eight, Mary's dressmaker and close
friend, holding a dark blue velvet bodice embroidered with
jet beads.

LINCOLN

It's late, Mrs. Keckley.

ELIZABETH KECKLEY
(holding out the bodice:)
She needs this for the grand reception.

Lincoln bends down to look at the intricate beading.

ELIZABETH KECKLEY

It's slow work.

He nods, smiles, straightens up.

> LINCOLN
>
> Good night.

He continues down the hall. Mrs. Keckley starts to enter Mary's boudoir, then stops, sensing something amiss. She calls quietly after Lincoln:

> ELIZABETH KECKLEY
> (concerned, a little exasperated:)
> Did you tell her a dream?

INT. LINCOLN'S OFFICE, SECOND FLOOR, WHITE HOUSE—NIGHT

A working room, sparsely furnished. Lincoln's desk is heaped with files, books, newspapers. The desk's near a window, now open. Comfortable chairs and a rocker are in a corner. Near the fireplace, in which embers are dying, there's a long table, eight chairs around it, settings by each chair of inkwells and pens.

Dozens of maps cover the walls and crowded bookcases.

Lincoln opens the door and enters to find his ten-year-old son TAD LINCOLN near the hearth, sleeping, sprawled on a very large military map. Lead toy soldiers are scattered across it.

A large mahogany box, imprinted "Alexander Gardner Studios," is open near Tad's head. The box contains large glass plates, each framed in wood; these are photographic negatives. Tad's been looking at several, which lie near him on the map.

Lincoln kneels by Tad and looks down at the map, a topo-
graphical and strategic survey of the no-man's land between
Union and Confederate forces at Petersburg. He scrutinizes
the precisely drawn blue and gray lines.

He lifts one of the glass plates and holds it to the firelight:
it's a large photographic negative of a young black boy. There's
a caption, in elegant cursive script: "Abner, age 12—$500."

And another: "Two young boys, 10 and 14—$700."

Lincoln puts the plates back in the box and closes the lid.
Carefully brushing the toy soldiers aside, he lies down beside
Tad. He touches Tad's hair and kisses his forehead. Tad stirs
as Lincoln gets on all fours; without really waking up, knowing
the routine, Tad climbs onto his father's back. Tad holds on as
his father stands, weary, and maybe a little surprised to find his
growing son slightly heavier than he was the night before.

TAD

(fast asleep:)
Papa . . .

LINCOLN

Hmm?

TAD

Papa I wanna see Willie.

LINCOLN

(whispering:)
Me, too, Taddie. But we can't.

TAD

Why not?

LINCOLN

Willie's gone. Three years now. He's gone.

Lincoln carries Tad out of the room, closing the door.

EXT. OUTSIDE THE TREASURY DEPARTMENT,
WASHINGTON—MORNING

A new flagpole is being dedicated. Lincoln, in a black over-
coat and his stovepipe hat, and Treasury Secretary WILLIAM
FESSENDEN, fifty-nine, stand by the pole. They face an
AUDIENCE of officials, clerks, dignitaries, wives, soldiers. A
MARINE BAND finishes a jaunty instrumental rendition of
"We Are Coming Father Abra'am."

TWO SOLDIERS fasten a flag to the halyards. Lincoln
moves into place; as the crowd applauds, he takes a sheet of
paper from inside his hat and glances at it. Then he looks up.

> LINCOLN
> The part assigned to me is to raise the flag,
> which, if there be no fault in the machinery,
> I will do, and when up, it will be for the
> people to keep it up.

He puts the paper away. The audience waits, expecting more.

> LINCOLN
> That's my speech.

He smiles at them. They applaud, some laughing. As Lincoln turns the crank, hoisting the flag, a solo trumpet plays
"We Are Coming Father Abra'am" and the audience joins in.
Among them, Secretary of State WILLIAM SEWARD, sixty-
four, in a thick, exquisite winter coat and hat, and Lincoln's
dapper assistant secretary, JOHN HAY, twenty-seven. Seward
looks pleased.

                    AUDIENCE
"We are coming, Father Abra'am,
three hundred thousand more,
From Mississippi's winding stream
and from New England's shore . . .
We leave our plows and workshops,
our wives and children dear,
With hearts too full for utterance,
With but a silent tear.
We're coming Father Abra'am . . ."

EXT. A CARRIAGE, PENNSYLVANIA AVENUE,
WASHINGTON—MORNING

In a four-door carriage, top down, Seward sits opposite Lincoln. Hay, next to Seward, organizes papers in a portfolio on his lap.

                    SEWARD
Even if every Republican in the House
votes yes—far from guaranteed, since when
has our party unanimously supported anything?—but say all our fellow Republicans
vote for it. We'd still be twenty votes short.

                    LINCOLN
Only twenty.

                    SEWARD
Only twenty!

                    LINCOLN
We can find twenty votes.

                    SEWARD
Twenty House Democrats who'll vote to
abolish slavery! In my opinion—

LINCOLN
To which I always listen.

SEWARD
Or pretend to.

LINCOLN
With all three of my ears.

SEWARD
We'll win the war soon—it's inevitable, isn't it?

LINCOLN
Ain't won yit.

SEWARD
You'll begin your second term with semi-
divine stature. Imagine the possibilities
peace will bring! Why tarnish your invalu-
able luster with a battle in the *House*? It's
a rats' nest in there, the same gang of tal-
entless hicks and hacks that rejected the
amendment ten months back. We'll lose.

Lincoln smiles.

LINCOLN
I like our chances now.

INT. LINCOLN'S OFFICE, THE WHITE HOUSE—MORNING

Lincoln is at his desk, Hay feeding him documents to read
and sign. Seward warms himself by the fireplace, holding a
brandy.

SEWARD

Consider the obstacles that we'd face. The
aforementioned two-thirds majority needed
to pass an amendment: we have a Republican majority, but barely more than fifty
percent—

LINCOLN

Fifty-six.

SEWARD

We need Democratic support. There's none
to be had.

LINCOLN

Since the House last voted on the amendment there's been an election. Sixty-four
Democrats lost their House seats in Novem-
ber. That's sixty-four Democrats looking for
work come March.

SEWARD	LINCOLN
I know, but that's—	They don't need to worry about reelection, they can vote however it suits 'em.

There's a knock at the office door.

SEWARD	LINCOLN
But we can't, um, *buy* the vote for the amendment. It's too important.	(to Hay:) Might as well let 'em in.

LINCOLN

I said nothing of buying anything. We need
twenty votes was all I said. Start of my second term, plenty of positions to fill.

Hay opens the door to the outer office, admitting the sound of a sizable crowd. JOHN NICOLAY, thirty-three, Lincoln's rather severe German-born senior secretary, ushers in MR. JOLLY, mid-forties, mud-spattered coat, hat in hands, followed by MRS. JOLLY, similarly road-worn, holding a suitcase. Lincoln stands.

> JOHN NICOLAY
> Mr. President, may I present Mr. and Mrs.
> Jolly who've come from Missouri to—

> MR. JOLLY
> From Jeff City, President.

Lincoln shakes Mr. Jolly's hand. Mrs. Jolly curtseys.

> LINCOLN
> Mr. Jolly. Ma'am. This by the fire's Secretary
> of State Seward.

Seward nods slightly as he lights a Cuban cigar.

> LINCOLN
> Jeff City.

Lincoln looks at the Jollys. They are worried and a little awed.

> LINCOLN
> I heard tell once of a Jefferson City lawyer
> who had a parrot that'd wake him each
> morning crying out, "Today is the day the
> world shall end, as scripture has foretold."
> And one day the lawyer shot him for the
> sake of peace and quiet, I presume, thus
> fulfilling, for the bird at least, its prophecy!

Lincoln smiles. The Jollys don't get it. Mr. Jolly looks back at Seward, who gestures for him to speak, then exhales a plume of smoke.

MR. JOLLY
(launching into his prepared speech:)
They's only one tollbooth in Jeff City, t' the
southwest 'n' this man Heinz Sauermagen
from Rolla been in illegal possession for
near two yar, since your man General Scho-
field set him up there. But President Monroe give that tollgate to my granpap and
Quincy Adams give my pap a letter saying
it's our'n for keeps. Mrs. Jolly got the—
(to his wife:)
Show Mr. Lincoln the Quincy Adams letter.

Mrs. Jolly opens the suitcase and begins to dig frantically for
the letter.

LINCOLN
That's unnecessary, Mrs. Jolly. Just tell me
what you want from me.

Seward exhales more smoke. Mr. Jolly starts coughing, while
Mrs. Jolly tries to fan away the cigar smoke with the Quincy
Adams letter.

MRS. JOLLY
Mr. Jolly's emphysema don't care for cigars.

SEWARD
Madam. Do you know about the proposed
Thirteenth Amendment to the Constitution—

MRS. JOLLY
Yes sir, everybody knows of it. The president
favors it.

SEWARD
Do you?

MRS. JOLLY
We do.

SEWARD
You know that it abolishes slavery?

MRS. JOLLY
Yes sir. I know it.

SEWARD
And is that why you favor it?

MRS. JOLLY
What I favor's ending the war. Once't we
do away with slavery, the rebs'll quit fighting, since slavery's what they're fighting for.
Mr. Lincoln, you always says so. With the
amendment, slavery's ended and they'll give
up. The war can finish then.

SEWARD
If the war finished first, before we end slavery, would—

MRS. JOLLY
President Lincoln says the war won't stop
unless we finish slavery—

SEWARD
But if it did. The South is exhausted. If they
run out of bullets and men, would you still
want your, uh— Who's your representative?

LINCOLN
Jeff City? That's, uh, Congressman Burton?

MRS. JOLLY
"Beanpole" Burton, I mean, Josiah Burton,
yes, sir!

LINCOLN
(to Mrs. Jolly:)
Republican. Undecided on the question
of the amendment, I believe. Perhaps you
could call on him and inform him of your
enthusiasm.

MRS. JOLLY
Yeah . . .

SEWARD
Madam? If the rebels surrender next week,
would you, at the end of this month, want
Congressman Burton to vote for the Thirteenth Amendment?

Mrs. Jolly is puzzled, and looks to Mr. Jolly. Then:

MRS. JOLLY
If that was how it was, no more war and all,
I reckon Mr. Jolly'd much prefer *not* to have
Congress pass the amendment.

Mr. Jolly nods. Seward glances at Lincoln, then turns back to
the Jollys:

SEWARD
And why's that?

Mr. Jolly's surprised: the answer's so obvious.

MR. JOLLY
(in a hoarse voice:)
Niggers.

MRS. JOLLY
If he don't have to let some Alabama coon
come up to Missouri, steal his chickens, and
his job, he'd much prefer that.

Seward takes the letter from Mrs. Jolly and hands it to Lincoln.

>SEWARD
>(to Lincoln, quietly:)
>The people!
>I begin to see why you're in such a great
>hurry to put it through.

>LINCOLN
>(to Mr. Jolly:)
>Would you let me study this letter, sir, about
>the tollbooth? Come back to me in the morn-
>ing and we'll consider what the law says.

Lincoln stands.

>LINCOLN
>And be sure to visit "Beanpole" and tell
>him that you support passage of the amend-
>ment. As a military necessity.

The Jollys nod, skeptical now.

>JOHN NICOLAY
>(to the Jollys:)
>Thank you.

Nicolay escorts them out. Before he closes the door:

>LINCOLN
>Oh, Nicolay? When you have a moment.

Nicolay nods and steps into the anteroom, where dozens
more petitioners are waiting to speak with Lincoln. Hay con-
fers with the doorman. Seward closes the door behind them.

Lincoln kneels at the fireplace, stoking the fire. He puts
more wood in, then stands. Seward watches him, then:

SEWARD

If procuring votes with offers of employ-
ment is what you intend, I'll fetch a friend
from Albany who can supply the skulking
men gifted at this kind of shady work. Spare
me the indignity of actually speaking to
Democrats. Spare you the exposure and
liability.

There is a sharp knock on the closed door, followed by two
long ones.

LINCOLN

Pardon me, that's a distress signal, which
I am bound by solemn oath to respond to.

Lincoln opens the door. Tad enters, cross.

TAD

Tom Pendel took away the glass camera
plates of slaves Mr. Gardner sent over
because Tom says Mama says they're too
distressing, but—

LINCOLN

You had nightmares all night, Mama's right
to—

TAD

But I'll have worse nightmares if you don't
let me look at the plates again!

LINCOLN

Perhaps.

SEWARD

We can't afford a single defection from
anyone in our party . . . not even a single

Republican absent when they vote. You
know who you've got to see.

Nicolay enters. Lincoln turns to him.

LINCOLN
Send over to Blair House. Ask Preston Blair
can I call on him around five o'clock.

SEWARD
(a shudder, a swallow of brandy:)
God help you. God alone knows what he'll
ask you to give him.

INT. THE LIBRARY, BLAIR HOUSE, WASHINGTON—
EVENING

Lincoln's perched on the edge of an ottoman.

LINCOLN
If the Blairs tell 'em to, no Republican will
balk at voting for the amendment.

The room is baronial. PRESTON BLAIR, patriarch of his
wealthy and powerful family, seventy-two years old, sits facing his son, MONTGOMERY BLAIR, fifty, whip-thin. A fire
blazes in a massive fireplace behind Monty. Preston's handsome, elegant daughter, ELIZABETH BLAIR LEE, forty-five,
sits across from Monty, next to Tad, who's wearing a Union
infantryman's uniform, a real musket by his side.

MONTGOMERY BLAIR
No conservative Republican is what you
mean—

PRESTON BLAIR

All Republicans ought to be conservative,
I founded this party—in my own goddamned
home—to be a *conservative* antislavery party,
not a hobbyhorse for goddamned radical
abolitionists and—

ELIZABETH BLAIR LEE

Damp down the dyspepsia, Daddy, you'll
frighten the child.

MONTGOMERY BLAIR
(to Lincoln:)

You need us to keep the conservative side of
the party in the traces while you diddle the
radicals and bundle up with Thaddeus
Stevens's gang. You need our help.

LINCOLN

Yes, sir, I do.

MONTGOMERY BLAIR

Well, what do we get?

ELIZABETH BLAIR LEE

Whoo! Blunt! Your manners, Monty, must
be why Mr. Lincoln pushed you out of his
cabinet.

PRESTON BLAIR	MONTGOMERY BLAIR
He was pushed out—	I wasn't pushed.

ELIZABETH BLAIR LEE
(smiling sarcastically:)

Oh of course you weren't.

PRESTON BLAIR	MONTGOMERY BLAIR
He was pushed out to placate the	(to Tad:)
goddamn radical abolitionists!	I agreed to resign.

ELIZABETH BLAIR LEE
(a nod at Tad:)
Oh Daddy, please!

PRESTON BLAIR
You don't mind, boy, do you?

LINCOLN
He spends his days with soldiers.

TAD
They taught me a song!

PRESTON BLAIR
Did they? Soldiers know all manner of
songs. How's your brother Bob?

TAD
He's at school now, but he's coming to visit
in four days! For the shindy!

PRESTON BLAIR
At school! Ain't that fine! Good he's not in
the Army!

TAD
Oh he wants to be, but Mama said he can't—

PRESTON BLAIR
Dangerous life, soldiering.

ELIZABETH BLAIR LEE
Your mama is wise to keep him clean out of
that.

PRESTON BLAIR
Now your daddy knows that what I want,
in return for all the help I give him, is to

go down to Richmond like he said I could,
soon as Savannah fell, and talk to Jefferson
Davis. Give me terms I can offer to Jefferson
Davis to start negotiating for peace. He'll
talk to me!

MONTGOMERY BLAIR
Conservative members of your party want
you to listen to overtures from Richmond.
That above all.

TWO BLACK SERVANTS who have entered begin to pour
and serve tea.

MONTGOMERY BLAIR
They'll vote for this rash and dangerous
amendment only if every other possibility is
exhausted.

PRESTON BLAIR
Our Republicans ain't abolitionists. We
can't tell our people they can vote yes on
abolishing slavery unless at the same time
we can tell 'em that you're seeking a negoti-
ated peace.

The Blairs look at Lincoln, waiting for an answer.

EXT. OUTSIDE BLAIR HOUSE—NIGHT

A light snow's beginning to fall. A lacquered coach stands
outside the house, the Blair crest in gold on its doors.

Elizabeth Blair Lee, a blanket in her arms, comes out of the
house, talking to LEO, an elderly black servant, formerly a
slave belonging to the Blairs. They're followed by MINERVA,
an elderly black woman in a housekeeper's uniform.

> ELIZABETH BLAIR LEE
> Leo, it's a hundred miles to Richmond. Get
> him drunk so he can sleep.

> LEO
> Yes'm.

Elizabeth goes to the carriage, where Preston awaits. She
passes the blanket through the carriage window and tucks it
around her father.

> ELIZABETH BLAIR LEE
> Here, Daddy.

> PRESTON BLAIR   ELIZABETH BLAIR LEE
> Oh! Thank you.   (fussing with the blanket:)
>   Let's fix this up . . .

> PRESTON BLAIR
> Where's my hat?

> ELIZABETH BLAIR LEE
> Leo has your hat. All right?

As Leo climbs into the carriage, Elizabeth kisses her hand,
then slaps the kiss on her father's cheek.

> ELIZABETH BLAIR LEE
> Go make peace.

INT. LINCOLN'S OFFICE, WHITE HOUSE—MORNING

The cabinet has assembled. Lincoln heads the table, Seward
at his left and EDWIN M. STANTON, Secretary of War, fifty-
one, barrel-shaped, long-bearded, bespectacled, at his right.
Next to him are Secretary of the Navy GIDEON WELLES,
sixty-three, luxurious white hair (it's a wig) and a flowing

snowy beard; Postmaster General WILLIAM DENNISON, fifty; Secretary of the Interior JOHN USHER, forty-nine; Secretary of the Treasury WILLIAM FESSENDEN, fifty-nine; and Attorney General JAMES SPEED, fifty-three.

Nicolay and Hay are in chairs behind Lincoln, taking notes.

LINCOLN
(to Stanton:)
Thunder forth, God of War!

STANTON
(clears his throat:)
We'll commence our assault on Wilmington from the sea.
(peeved; he's noted a singed edge of the map:)
Why is this burnt? Was the boy playing with it?

LINCOLN
It got took by a breeze several nights back.

STANTON
This is an official War Department map!

SEWARD
And the entire cabinet's waiting to hear what it portends.

WELLES
A bombardment. From the largest fleet the Navy has ever assembled.

LINCOLN
(to Welles:)
Old Neptune! Shake thy hoary locks!

Welles stands.

WELLES

Fifty-eight ships are underway, of every ton-
nage and firing range.

Welles gestures on the map to the positions of many ships.

STANTON

We'll keep up a steady barrage. Our first target is Fort Fisher. It defends Wilmington port.

Stanton indicates the lines tracing artillery trajectories.
These converge particularly heavily on Fort Fisher.

JAMES SPEED

A steady barrage?

STANTON

A hundred shells a minute.

There's a moment of shocked silence.

STANTON

Till they surrender.

WILLIAM FESSENDEN

Dear God.

WELLES

Yes. Yes.

LINCOLN

Wilmington's their last open seaport.
Therefore . . .

STANTON

Wilmington falls, Richmond falls after.

SEWARD

And the war . . . is done.

The rest of the cabinet applauds, foot stomping, table slapping. Only John Usher doesn't join in.

JOHN USHER
Then why, if I may ask are we not concentrating the nation's attention on Wilmington? Why, instead, are we reading in the *Herald*—

(he smacks a newspaper on the table:)
—that the anti-slavery amendment is being precipitated onto the House floor for debate—because *your* eagerness, in what seems an unwarranted intrusion of the Executive into Legislative prerogatives, is compelling it to its . . . to what's likely to be its premature demise? You signed the Emancipation Proclamation, you've done all that can be expected—

JAMES SPEED
The Emancipation Proclamation's merely a war measure. After the war the courts'll make a meal of it.

JOHN USHER
(to Lincoln:)
When Edward Bates was Attorney General, he felt confident in it enough to allow you to sign—

JAMES SPEED
(a shrug:)
Different lawyers, different opinions. It frees slaves as a military exigent, not in any other—

LINCOLN
I don't recall Bates being any too certain about the legality of my Proclamation, just

it wasn't downright criminal. Somewhere's in between. Back when I rode the legal circuit in Illinois I defended a woman from Metamora named Melissa Goings, seventy-seven years old, they said she murdered her husband; he was eighty-three. He was choking her; and, uh, she grabbed ahold of a stick of firewood and fractured his skull, 'n' he died. In his will he wrote, "I expect she has killed me. If I get over it, I will have revenge."

This gets a laugh.

LINCOLN
No one was keen to see her convicted, he was that kind of husband. I asked the prosecuting attorney if I might have a short conference with my client. And she and I went into a room in the courthouse, but I alone emerged. The window in the room was found to be wide open. It was believed the old lady may have climbed out of it. I told the bailiff right before I left her in the room she asked me where she could get a good drink of water, and I told her Tennessee. Mrs. Goings was seen no more in Metamora. Enough justice had been done; they even forgave the bondsman her bail.

JOHN USHER
I'm afraid I don't—

LINCOLN
I decided that the Constitution gives me war powers, but no one knows just exactly what those powers are. Some say they don't exist. I don't know. I decided I needed

them to exist to uphold my oath to protect
the Constitution, which I decided meant
that I could take the rebels' slaves from 'em
as property confiscated in war. That might
recommend to suspicion that I agree with
the rebs that their slaves are property in the
first place. Of course I don't, never have,
I'm glad to see any man free, and if calling
a man property, or war contraband, does
the trick . . . Why I caught at the opportu-
nity. Now here's where it gets truly slippery.
I use the law allowing for the seizure of
property in a war knowing it applies only to
the property of governments and citizens
of belligerent nations. But the South ain't
a nation, that's why I can't negotiate with
'em. So *if* in fact the Negroes *are* property
according to law, have I the right to take the
rebels' property from 'em, if I insist they're
rebels only, and not citizens of a belligerent
country? And slipperier still: I maintain it
ain't our actual Southern states in rebel-
lion, but only the rebels living in those
states, the laws of which states remain in
force. *The laws of which states remain in force.*
That means, that since it's states' laws that
determine whether Negroes can be sold as
slaves, as property—the federal government
doesn't have a say in that, least not yet—

(a glance at Seward, then:)

—then Negroes in those states are slaves,
hence property, hence my war powers allow
me to confiscate 'em as such. So I confiscated 'em. But if I'm a respecter of states'
laws, how then can I legally free 'em with
my Proclamation, as I done, unless I'm can-
celing states' laws? I felt the war demanded
it; my oath demanded it; I felt right with

myself; and I hoped it was legal to do it, I'm
hoping still.

He looks around the table. Everyone's listening.

> LINCOLN
> Two years ago I proclaimed these people
> emancipated—"then, thenceforward and
> forever free." But let's say the courts decide
> I had no authority to do it. They might well
> decide that. Say there's no amendment
> abolishing slavery. Say it's after the war, and
> I can no longer use my war powers to just
> ignore the courts' decisions, like I some-
> times felt I had to do. Might those people
> I freed be ordered back into slavery? That's
> why I'd like to get the Thirteenth Amend-
> ment through the House, and on its way
> to ratification by the states, wrap the whole
> slavery thing up, forever and aye. As soon as
> I'm able. *Now.* End of this month. And I'd
> like you to stand behind me. Like my cabi-
> net's most always done.

A moment's silence, broken by a sharp laugh from Seward.

> LINCOLN
> As the preacher said, I could write shorter
> sermons but once I start I get too lazy to
> stop.

> JOHN USHER
> It seems to me, sir, you're describing pre-
> cisely the sort of dictator the Democrats
> have been howling about.

> JAMES SPEED
> Dictators aren't susceptible to law.

JOHN USHER

Neither is he! He just said as much! Ignor-
ing the courts? Twisting meanings? What
reins him in from, from . . .

LINCOLN

Well, the people do that, I suppose. I signed
the Emancipation Proclamation a year and
half before my second election. I felt I was
within my power to do it; however I also felt
that I might be wrong about that; I knew
the people would tell me. I gave 'em a year
and half to think about it. And they re-
elected me.
    (Beat.)
And come February the first, I intend to
sign the Thirteenth Amendment.

INT. LINCOLN'S OFFICE, WHITE HOUSE—EARLY
AFTERNOON

Nicolay opens the door to the crowded outer office to admit
perpetually worried JAMES ASHLEY, forty-two (R, OH). Tad
eyes him from a chair by the window.

Lincoln enters the room with Seward.

LINCOLN

Well, Mr. Representative Ashley! Tell us the
news from the Hill.

Lincoln shakes his hand and warmly claps the discombobu-
lated but flattered representative on the shoulder.

JAMES ASHLEY

Well! Ah! News—

LINCOLN
Why for instance is this thus, and what is
the reason for this thusness?

JAMES ASHLEY
I . . .

SEWARD
James, we want you to bring the anti-slavery
amendment to the floor for debate—

JAMES ASHLEY
Excuse me. *What?*

SEWARD
—immediately, and— You are
the amendment's manager,
are you not?

JAMES ASHLEY
I am, of course—but—
Immediately?

SEWARD
And we're counting on robust radical support, so tell Mr. Stevens we expect him to
put his back into it, it's not going to be easy,
but we trust—

JAMES ASHLEY
It's *impossible.* No, I am sorry, no, we can't
organize anything *immediately* in the House.
I have been canvassing the Democrats since
the election, in case any of them softened
after they got walloped. But they have
stiffened if anything, Mr. Secretary. There
aren't nearly enough votes—

LINCOLN
We're whalers, Mr. Ashley!

JAMES ASHLEY
Whalers? As in, um, whales?

Lincoln moves in, standing very close to Ashley.

LINCOLN

We've been chasing this whale for a long
time. We've finally placed a harpoon in the
monster's back. It's *in*, James, it's in! We
finish the deed now, we can't wait! Or with
one flop of his tail he'll smash the boat and
send us all to eternity!

SEWARD

On the thirty-first of this month. Of this
year. Put the amendment up for a vote.

Ashley is agog.

INT. THADDEUS STEVENS'S OFFICE IN THE CAPITOL—
EVENING

The room's redolent of politics, ideology (a bust of Robespi-
erre, a print of Tom Paine), long occupancy and hard work.
On the wall opposite a massive desk hangs a faded banner:
"Reelect Thaddeus Stevens, Republican Ticket, 9th Congressional District, Lancaster, Pennsylvania." At the desk sits
THADDEUS STEVENS (R, PA), seventy-three, bald under
a horrible red wig, a gaunt, powerful face resembling Lincoln's, though beardless and bitter.

In the office are Ashley, Speaker of the House SCHUYLER
COLFAX (R, IN), formidable Senator BLUFF WADE (R, MA),
who's never smiled, and ASA VINTNER LITTON (R, MD).

BLUFF WADE

Whalers?

JAMES ASHLEY

That's what he said.

BLUFF WADE

The man's never been near a whale ship in
his life!
  (to Stevens:)
Withdraw radical support, force him to
abandon this scheme, whatever he's up to.
—He drags his feet about everything, Lincoln; why this urgency? We got it through
the Senate without difficulty because we had
the numbers. Come December you'll have
the same in the House. The amendment'll
be the easy work of ten minutes.

ASA VINTNER LITTON

He's using the *threat* of the amendment to
frighten the rebels into an immediate surrender.

SCHUYLER COLFAX

I imagine we'd rejoice to see that.

ASA VINTNER LITTON

Will you rejoice when the Southern states
have rejoined the Union, pell-mell, as Lincoln intends them to, and one by one each
refuses to ratify the amendment? *If* we pass
it, which we won't.
  (to Stevens:)
Why are we cooperating with, with *him?* We
all know what he's doing and we all know
what he'll do. We can't offer up abolition's
best legal prayer to his games and tricks.

BLUFF WADE

He's said he'd welcome the South back with
all its slaves in chains.

JAMES ASHLEY
Three years ago he said that! To calm the
border states when we were—

THADDEUS STEVENS
I don't.

This confuses the room. Stevens turns to Litton.

THADDEUS STEVENS
You said, "We all know what he'll do."
I don't know.

ASA VINTNER LITTON
You know he isn't to be trusted.

THADDEUS STEVENS
Trust? I'm sorry, I was under the misappre-
hension your chosen profession was politics.
I've never trusted the president. I never trust
anyone. But . . . Hasn't he surprised you?

ASA VINTNER LITTON
No, Mr. Stevens, he hasn't.

THADDEUS STEVENS
Nothing surprises you, Asa, therefore nothing about you is surprising. Perhaps that is
why your constituents did not reelect you to
the coming term.
(collecting his cane and standing:)
It's late, I'm old, I'm going home.

Stevens limps to the door, opens it, and turns.

THADDEUS STEVENS
Lincoln the inveterate dawdler, Lincoln the
Southerner, Lincoln the capitulating com-

promiser, our adversary—and leader of the
godforsaken Republican Party, *our* party—
Abraham Lincoln has asked us to work with
him to accomplish the death of slavery in
America.
　　(Beat.)
Retain, even in opposition, your capacity
for astonishment.

Stevens leaves, shutting the door. They watch him go, Ashley
excited, Litton unmoved, insulted, skeptical.

INT. PRIVATE DINING ROOM, OLD TAVERN IN
WASHINGTON—NIGHT

In a cramped private alcove, a low, sagging timber ceiling,
sooty walls, sawdusted floor, ancient curtain closing it off,
Seward sits at a small table with ROBERT LATHAM, an
Albany, NY, political operative; RICHARD SCHELL, a Wall
Street speculator; and W. N. BILBO, a Tennessee lawyer and
lobbyist. A chandelier with candles drips wax on them.

On the table, a leather folio lies open: prospectuses for jobs
in the administration. Latham and Schell study these. Bilbo
is studying Seward.

> SEWARD
> The president is never to be mentioned.
> Nor I. You're paid for your discretion.

> W. N. BILBO
> Hell, you can have that for nothin', what we
> need money for is bribes. It'd speed things
> up.

> SEWARD
> No. Nothing strictly illegal.

ROBERT LATHAM

It's not illegal to bribe congressmen. They
starve otherwise.

RICHARD SCHELL

I have explained to Mr. Bilbo and Mr. Latham
that we're offering patronage jobs to the
Dems who vote yes. Jobs and nothing more.

SEWARD

That's correct.

W. N. BILBO

Congressmen come cheap! Few thousand
bucks'll buy you all you need.

SEWARD

The president would be unhappy to hear
you did that.

W. N. BILBO

Well, will he be unhappy if we lose?

A WAITRESS brings in a platter of roasted crabs, which she
slams down on the table, and leaves.

SEWARD

The money I managed to raise for this
endeavor is only for your fees, food and
lodgings.

W. N. BILBO

Uh-huh. If that squirrel-infested attic you've
quartered us in's any measure, you ain't
raised much.

RICHARD SCHELL

Shall we get to work?

Bilbo takes a mallet to a crab, smashing it!

INT. FLOOR OF THE HOUSE OF REPRESENTATIVES—
DAY

A gavel slams down on a sounding block in an attempt to silence the raucous tumult in the large chamber. It subsides enough for Colfax to be heard from his chair atop the central dais:

> SCHUYLER COLFAX
> The House recognizes Fernando Wood, the honorable representative from New York.

TITLE:
**THE HOUSE DEBATE BEGINS
JANUARY 9**

Floor and balcony are full, although the desks of representatives from seceded states are bare and unoccupied.

On the Democratic side, 81 members applaud FERNANDO WOOD (D, NY) as he takes the podium. The Democratic leadership, including GEORGE YEAMAN (KY), has gathered around House minority leader GEORGE PENDLETON (OH). On the Republican side of the aisle, enraged booing from the 102 Republicans, including HIRAM PRICE (IA), GEORGE JULIAN (IN), Litton and Ashley, all gathered around Stevens's desk.

> FERNANDO WOOD
> Estimable colleagues. Two bloody years ago this month, His Highness, King Abraham Africanus the First—our Great Usurping Caesar, violator of habeas corpus and freedom of the press, abuser of states' rights—

HIRAM PRICE	FERNANDO WOOD
(loud:)	—radical Republican autocrat
If Lincoln really were a tyrant,	ruling by fiat and martial law
Mr. Wood, he'd'a had your	affixed his name to his
empty head impaled on a pike,	heinous and illicit
and the country better for it!	Emancipation Proclamation,
	promising it would hasten
	the end of the war, which yet
	rages on and on.

Murmuring from the floor and the balcony, in the front row of which Mary and Elizabeth Keckley sit. Mary turns her gaze from the floor to watch Latham and Schell, a few seats away, scrutinize the floor, whispering, Latham taking notes. Schell holds the leather prospectus folio in his lap. Bilbo sits behind them.

They study the other New York Democrats—CHARLES HANSON, NELSON MERRICK, HENRY LANFORD, HOMER BENSON, GILES STUART—who comprise a cluster of glum uncomfortable passivity on that side of the aisle.

FERNANDO WOOD	ROBERT LATHAM
He claimed, as tyrants do,	(whispering to Schell:)
that the war's emergencies	The New York delegation's
permitted him to turn our	looking decidedly uninspired.
Army into the unwilling	
instrument of his monarch-	
ical ambitions—	

Wood points at Stevens, granite-faced. Stevens's eyes burn back at Wood.

FERNANDO WOOD
—and radical Republicanism's abolitionist
fanaticism!

This prompts shouts and boos from the Republicans.

FERNANDO WOOD
His Emancipation Proclamation has obliterated millions of dollars' worth of personal
property rights—

Schell examines the Pennsylvania Democrats: an openly
appalled ARCHIBALD MORAN, AMBROSE BAILER and,
chewing his thumb, a painful fake grin pinned to his face,
ALEXANDER COFFROTH. Schell leans in to Latham.

FERNANDO WOOD
—and "liberated" the hundreds
of thousands of hopelessly
indolent Negro refugees, bred
by nature for servility, to settle
in squalor in our Northern
cities!

RICHARD SCHELL
Over in Pennsylvania—
who's the sweaty man
eating his thumb?

ROBERT LATHAM
Unknown to me. Seems
jumpy.

RICHARD SCHELL
Perhaps he'll jump.

Cheering and booing.

In the Connecticut delegation, JOHN ELLIS (D) winds
his pocket watch, looking contemptuously at Wood. Schell
makes a note.

FERNANDO WOOD
But all that was not enough for
this dictator, who now seeks to
insinuate his miscegenist
pollution into the Constitution
itself!

W. N. BILBO
Jesus, when's this son-of-
liberty sonofabitch
gonna sit down?

RICHARD SCHELL
John Ellis is going
to break his watch
if he doesn't stop—

FERNANDO WOOD

We are once again asked—nay, com-
manded—to consider a proposed thirteenth amendment which, if passed, shall
set at immediate liberty four million col-
oreds while manacling the limbs of the
white race in America. *If it is passed—but it
shall not pass!*

Wild cheering and booing.

FERNANDO WOOD	ROBERT LATHAM
Every member of the House loyal to the Democratic Party and the constituents it serves shall oppose—	What's more interesting is how dismal and disgruntled Mr. Yeaman appears. He should be cheering right now, but . . .

W. N. BILBO
Looks like he ate a bad oyster.

Thaddeus Stevens calls out from his desk.

THADDEUS STEVENS
A point of order, Mr. Speaker, if you please?
When will Mr. Wood—

FERNANDO WOOD
Mr. Speaker, I still have the floor and the gentleman from Pennsylvania is out of order!

THADDEUS STEVENS
—when will Mr. Wood conclude his inter-
minable gabble? Some of us breathe oxygen,
and we find the mephitic fumes of his oratory
a lethal challenge to our pleural capacities.

Wild cheering, applause from the Republicans.

FERNANDO WOOD
We shall oppose this amendment, and
any legislation that so affronts natural law,
insulting to God as to man! Congress must
never declare equal those whom God created unequal!

The Democrats cheer. Mary watches with concern. Mrs.
Keckley is angry and uncomfortable.

THADDEUS STEVENS
Slavery is the only insult to natural law, you
fatuous nincompoop!

GEORGE PENDLETON
Order! Procedure! Mr. Speaker, Mr. Wood
has the floor!
    (to Stevens:)
Instruct us, Oh Great Commoner, what is
unnatural, in your opinion?
Niggrahs casting ballots? Niggrah representatives? Is that natural, Stevens? Intermarriage?

THADDEUS STEVENS
What violates natural law? Slavery, and *you*,
Pendleton, you insult God, you unnatural noise.

An avalanche of boos and cheers as Democrats surge toward
Wood, Republicans toward Stevens. Ashley rushes to Colfax,
calling:

JAMES ASHLEY
Mr. Colfax! Please, use your gavel! They are—
    (to the Democrats:)
You are out of order!
    (to Colfax:)
Direct the sergeant-at-arms to suppress this!
    (back to the Democrats:)
We are in session!

INT. SECOND FLOOR CORRIDOR OF THE WHITE
HOUSE—MORNING

The corridor as usual is lined with petitioners. They've lined
up along both sides of the wall and are hooting, laughing,
clapping and cheering, egging on Tad as, with furious concentration, he drives a cart pulled at considerable speed by
a large and seriously annoyed goat down the hall. White
House doorkeeper and unofficial child-minder TOM PEN-
DEL follows, admonishing the petitioners as he goes.

> TOM PENDEL
> Please don't encourage this! Don't encour-
> age this!

ROBERT LINCOLN, twenty-one, enters from the stairs
carrying several pieces of large and heavy luggage.

Tad sees him, jumps out of the goat cart, runs up to and
tackles Robert, causing him to drop his luggage. They
embrace as Pendel captures the goat and leads it away.

> TAD
> You're back you're back you're back you're
> back you're—

> ROBERT
> (laughing:)
> I am. Your goat got big.

Robert disentangles himself from Tad and hands him a suitcase.

> ROBERT
> Here, help me get one of these to my room.
> (a nervous glance at the door to Mary's
> bedroom suite:)
> Is she in there?

As Robert hoists the rest of the luggage himself, Tad chatters and a PETITIONER comes forward. He grabs the trunk as Robert's lifting it.

TAD
She's asleep, probably, they went to see Avonia Jones last night in a play about Israelites. Daddy's meeting with a famous scientist now and he's nervous because of how smart the man is and the man is angry about, 'cause there's a new book that Sam Beckwith says is about finches, and finches' beaks, about how they change, it takes years and years and years but—

PETITIONER
You need help, sir? I can . . .

ROBERT
No, sir, I don't. No.

PETITIONER
Could you bring your pa this letter I writ about my insolvency proceedings?

ROBERT
Let it go please, thank you. You deliver your own goddamned petition, thank you . . .

PETITIONER
Please, please.

Robert wrestles the trunk out of the man's grasp just as Mary enters the hall and sees him.

MARY
He's here . . .
    (calling down the hall:)
He's here, Mrs. Cuthbert! He's here!
    (to Robert:)
Robbie . . . Oh Robbie! Robbie!

> ROBERT
> (embracing her:)
> Hi, Mama. Hey. Hey . . .

> MARY
> (overjoyed:)
> Oh!

She instantly eyes Robert's amount of luggage with suspicion.

MARY	TAD
You're only staying a few days. Why'd you pack all of that?	—but what's made every one really cross with the man, the man who wrote the finch book, is he says people are cousins to monkeys, but he was going to say—
ROBERT	
Well, I don't know how long I'm—	

> MARY
> (to Tad:)
> Go tell your father Robert's home!

> TAD
> Mr. Nicolay says Daddy's secluded with Mr. Blair.

> MARY
> Tell him anyway.

Tad drops the suitcase and runs to the office. Mary strokes Robert's face, looking concerned.

> MARY
> You forget to eat, exactly like him.

> ROBERT
> (laughs:)
> No . . .

MARY
You'll linger a few days extra, after the
reception, before you go back to school.

ROBERT
Well, I don't know if I'm gonna go back to—

She stops him with an alarmed look.

MARY
We'll fatten you up before you return to
Boston.

ROBERT
All right, Mama.

MARY
All right.
            (beaming at him, adoringly:)
Oh Robbie . . .

INT. LINCOLN'S OFFICE, WHITE HOUSE—MORNING

Preston Blair, still in his traveling cloak, and Lincoln stand
near the fireplace facing one another.

PRESTON BLAIR
Jefferson Davis is sending three delegates:
Stephens, Hunter and Campbell: Vice
President of the Confederacy, their former
Secretary of State, and their Assistant Sec-
retary of War. They're coming in earnest to
propose peace.

Both men look into the fire. Preston moves closer.

PRESTON BLAIR

I know this is unwelcome news for you.
Now hear me: I went to Richmond to talk
to *traitors*, to smile at and plead with *traitors*,
because it'll be spring in two months, the
roads'll be passable, the spring slaughter
commences. Four bloody springs now!
Think of my Frank, who you've taken to
your heart, how you'll blame yourself if the
war takes my son as it's taken multitudes of
sons. Think of all the boys who'll die if you
don't make peace. You must talk with these
men!

LINCOLN

I intend to, Preston. And in return, I must
ask you—

PRESTON BLAIR	LINCOLN
No, this is *not* horsetrading, this is life and—	—to support our push for the amendment when it reaches the—

There's a knock on the door.

LINCOLN

Not now!

Robert enters. Nicolay stands behind him, apologetic.

LINCOLN

Oh. Bob. I'm sorry. Welcome home.

He shakes hands with his son, stiffly.

ROBERT

Thank you.

<table>
<tr><td>

LINCOLN
(to Robert:)
I'm talking to Preston Blair,
we—

</td><td>

PRESTON BLAIR
(pointedly:)
You're looking fit,
Robert. Harvard agrees
with you. Fit and rested.

</td></tr>
</table>

ROBERT

Mr. Blair.

LINCOLN
(dismissing Robert, unintentionally
abrupt:)
Just give us a moment please, Robert.
Thank you.

He turns to Preston. Robert, stung, hesitates, then leaves the room, Nicolay shutting the door behind him.

PRESTON BLAIR
I will procure your votes for you, as I prom-
ised. You've always kept your word to me.
Those Southern men are coming.
(taking Lincoln's hand:)
I beg you, in the name of gentle Christ—

<table>
<tr><td>

PRESTON BLAIR
Talk peace with these men.

</td><td>

LINCOLN
Preston, I understand . . .

</td></tr>
</table>

LINCOLN
(sharply:)
I understand, Preston.

EXT. ON THE MALL—AFTERNOON

JACOB GRAYLOR (D, PA) and Bilbo walk outside the Capitol. Graylor looks over the prospectuses.

ROBERT LATHAM (V.O.)
We have one abstention so far—

RICHARD SCHELL (V.O.)
Jacob Graylor—

Graylor selects one and hands it to Bilbo.

RICHARD SCHELL (V.O.)
He'd like to be Federal Revenue Assessor
for the Fifth District of Pennsylvania.

INT. A BEDROOM IN THE ST. CHARLES HOTEL—NIGHT

A small room, two beds, in disarray: newspapers, overflow-
ing ashtrays, whiskey bottles empty on the floor. Latham and
Schell stand at a table strewn with the remnants of a poker
game. Bilbo lies on one of the beds. All three are in their
shirtsleeves. Seward is at the table.

ROBERT LATHAM
—so the total of representatives voting
three weeks from today is reduced to 182,
which means 122 yes votes to reach the req-
uisite two-thirds of the House. Assuming all
Republicans vote for the amendment? . . .

Seward nods, less assertively than Latham would like.

ROBERT LATHAM
Then, despite our abstention, to reach a two-
thirds majority we remain 20 yeses short.

INT. THE OLD TAVERN, WASHINGTON—NIGHT

Bilbo is drinking schooners of beer with EDWIN LECLERK
(D, OH) and CLAY HAWKINS (D, OH). Hawkins listens as
Bilbo gives his pitch. LeClerk looks at the prospectuses.

ROBERT LATHAM (V.O.)
For which we're seeking from among 64
lame duck Democrats. Fully 39 of these we
deem unredeemable no votes.

LeClerk throws his beer in Bilbo's face, soaking Bilbo and the prospectuses. Hawkins looks shocked. LeClerk storms out.

INT. THE ROOM IN THE ST. CHARLES HOTEL—NIGHT

W. N. BILBO
The kind that hates niggers, hates God for
making niggers.

ROBERT LATHAM
The Good Lord on High would despair of
their souls.

SEWARD
(distastefully:)
Thank you for that pithy explanation, Mr.
Bilbo.

RICHARD SCHELL
We've abandoned these 39 to the Devil that
possesses them.

EXT. A WORKING-CLASS NEIGHBORHOOD IN
WASHINGTON—DAY

Schell stands at the door of a small, grubby row house. He presents the folio, warped from its beer bath, to WILLIAM HUTTON (D, IN), eyes red from crying, dressed in mourning black.

Hutton slams the door in Schell's face. A funeral wreath
that adorns the door falls to the ground. A daguerreotype
attached to the wreath depicts a young officer, Hutton's
brother Frederick.

INT. THE ROOM IN THE ST. CHARLES HOTEL—NIGHT

RICHARD SCHELL
The remaining lame ducks, on whom we've
been working with a purpose—

Schell hands Latham a stack of folded prospectuses, each
with a name scrawled on it.

ROBERT LATHAM
Charles Hanson.

EXT. IN FRONT OF THE CAPITOL—TWILIGHT

Representatives Merrick, Lanford, Benson, Stuart and Hanson, the New York lame ducks, descend the stairs, discussing
the opening of the amendment debate, to which they've just
been listening.

Latham smoothly holds Hanson back from the group, extend-
ing a hand, the still pristine portfolio under his arm. He
smiles as the other New York lame ducks proceed down the
stairs, unaware, then nods his head back up toward the Capitol steps, where Bilbo and Schell wait. Latham opens the
folio as he talks to Hanson.

INT. THE ROOM IN THE ST. CHARLES HOTEL—NIGHT

ROBERT LATHAM
Giles Stuart.

INT. THE TREASURY DEPARTMENT—DAY

In the grand lobby there are federal bank windows. Schell
is in line at one of these behind Giles Stuart, who completes
a transaction and leaves, counting money. Bilbo, barreling
the other way, intentionally slams into Stuart, causing him to
drop his money. Bilbo and Schell both kneel to help.

Schell places the open folio in Stuart's hands. As the men
pile his recovered money into the folio, Stuart's puzzled,
then intrigued. Schell gives him a meaningful look.

CLOSE ON A SMALL WOODEN FILE BOX

A folded prospectus, now with the name "Stuart" scrawled
on it, is added to a growing file.

INT. THE U.S. PATENT OFFICE, WASHINGTON—DAY

Visitors file past cabinets containing animal and plant speci-
mens and inventions; the line circles around a large case
in which an amputated leg capped with a brass plate is dis-
played. A sign identifies it: "Left Leg of General Daniel Sick-
les, at Gettysburg, July 5, 1863."

> ROBERT LATHAM (V.O.)
> Nelson Merrick.

Latham looks through the case at Schell, who's next to Nelson Merrick, who nods, solemnly staring at the leg. Schell
proffers Merrick the folio. Merrick flips through the folio.

> ROBERT LATHAM (V.O.)
> Homer Benson.

INT. A WORKINGMENS' LUNCHROOM, WASHINGTON—
DAY

A hall packed with working men, soaped-up windows. A
GYPSY FIDDLER saws away. Homer Benson, incongruous
in a suit, slurps. As he lifts his spoon to his mouth, the folio
is placed in front of him. He looks over, puzzled, as Schell
smiles and extends a hand.

Benson takes the folio. Schell slides his chair closer.

INT. THE ROOM IN THE ST. CHARLES HOTEL—NIGHT

Another prospectus joins the pile: "Benson"

                    ROBERT LATHAM
        And lastly . . .

Bilbo retrieves a paper from the floor and hands it to Seward.

                    W. N. BILBO
        Clay Hawkins. Of Ohio.

EXT. A WOODS ALONG THE POTOMAC RIVER—
MORNING

Bilbo walks with Clay Hawkins, who peruses the folio. Bilbo
has a small covered wicker basket slung over his shoulder.
Hawkins follows, happy and sick with fear.

                    CLAY HAWKINS
        T-tax collector for the Western Reserve.
        Th-th-that pays handsomely.

                    W. N. BILBO
        Don't just reach for the highest branches.
        They sway in every breeze. Assistant Port

Inspector of Marlston looks like the ticket
to me.

CLAY HAWKINS
Uh, boats, they, they make me sick.

Bilbo retrieves a snare; a small bird is trapped by the foot.
Bilbo stuffs the bird in the basket.

CLAY HAWKINS
So just stand on the dock. Let the Assistant
Assistant Port Inspector's stomach go weak.

Bilbo eyes Hawkins, who anxiously eyes the folio.

INT. LINCOLN'S OFFICE, WHITE HOUSE—EARLY
EVENING

Seward hands the last prospectus to Nicolay, who unfolds
it, places it on top of the other prospectuses, and records
details about Hawkins's appointment in a notebook. Seward
smokes a cigar, Nicolay a pipe. Lincoln sits, feet up, examining a newspaper.

SEWARD
And lastly, Democratic yes vote number six.
Hawkins from Ohio.

LINCOLN
Six.

SEWARD
Well, thus far. Plus Graylor's abstention.
From tiny acorns and so on.

LINCOLN
What'd Hawkins get?

JOHN NICOLAY
(still writing:)
Postmaster of the Millersburg Post Office.

LINCOLN
He's selling himself cheap, ain't he?

SEWARD
He wanted Tax Collector of the Western
Reserve—a first-term congressman who
couldn't manage reelection, I felt it unseemly
and they bargained him down to Postmaster.
(to Nicolay:)
Scatter 'em over several rounds of appoint-
ments, so no one notices. And burn this
ledger, please, after you're done.

Lincoln stands.

LINCOLN
(to Nicolay:)
Time for my public opinion bath. Might as
well let 'em in.

Nicolay helps Lincoln trade his shawl for his overcoat in
preparation to meet the public.

LINCOLN
Seven yeses with Mr. Ellis! Thirteen to go!

SEWARD
One last item, an absurdity, but—my associ-
ates report that among the Representatives
a fantastical rumor's bruited about, which
I immediately disavowed, that you'd allowed
bleary old Preston Blair to sojourn to Richmond to invite Jeff Davis to send commissioners up to Washington with a peace plan.

Lincoln is silent. A horrifying reality dawns for Seward:

> SEWARD
> I, of course, told them you would never . . .
> Not without consulting me, you wouldn't . . .
> Because why on earth would you?

EXT. IN AN OPEN FIELD NEAR PETERSBURG, VIRGINIA—
EVENING

THREE UNION CAVALRY OFFICERS consult with THREE
CONFEDERATE CAVALRY OFFICERS, all mounted. The
officers exchange documents and salutes.

TITLE:
NO MAN'S LAND
OUTSIDE PETERSBURG, VIRGINIA
JANUARY 11

The ranking Confederate trots to a buggy in which three
Confederate officials sit: Vice President ALEXANDER STE-
PHENS, fifty-three, short; JOHN A. CAMPBELL, Assistant
Secretary of War, fifty-four; and Senator R. M. T. HUNTER,
fifty-six. They're well-dressed for winter, Stephens especially
heavily bundled.

Stephens, Campbell and the indignant Hunter leave the
buggy and are escorted by Confederate officers to the waiting company of Union cavalry and infantry.

A Union Army ambulance, a large American flag painted on
one side, driven by TWO BLACK SOLDIERS, stands near
broken wagons and a derelict cannon. ANOTHER BLACK
SOLDIER stands at attention by the ambulance's rear door.

The soldier, staring coldly at these men, gestures brusquely
to the ambulance. The Confederate peace commissioners

hesitate; Hunter stares in horror at the black soldiers. Then
Stephens pushes past Hunter. He nods to the soldier.

> ALEXANDER STEPHENS
> (with polite dignity:)
> Much obliged.

He boards the ambulance. His fellow delegates follow in
his wake, Hunter glaring with defiant hatred at the soldiers
before climbing in.

INT. LINCOLN'S OFFICE, WHITE HOUSE—EARLY
EVENING

Seward stands, stunned. Lincoln sits at the cabinet table.
Nicolay is gone.

> SEWARD
> Why wasn't I consulted?! I'm Secretary of
> State! You, you, you informally send a reac-
> tionary dottard, to— What will happen, do
> you imagine, when these peace commission-
> ers arrive?

> LINCOLN
> We'll hear 'em out.

> SEWARD
> Oh, splendid! And next the Democrats will
> invite 'em up to hearings on the Hill, and
> the newspapers—well, the *newspapers*—the
> newspapers will ask, "Why risk enraging the
> Confederacy over the issue of slavery when
> they're here to make peace?" We'll lose
> every Democrat we've got, more than likely
> conservative Republicans will join 'em, and
> all our work, all our preparing the ground
> for the vote, laid waste, for naught.

LINCOLN

The Blairs have promised support for the
amendment if we listen to these people—

SEWARD

Oh, the Blairs promise, do they? You think
they'll keep their promise once we have
heard these delegates and refused them?
Which we will have to do, since their proposal most certainly will be predicated on
keeping their slaves!

LINCOLN

What hope for *any* Democratic votes, Willum, if word gets out that I've refused a
chance to end the war? You think word
won't get out? In Washington?

SEWARD

It's either the amendment or this Confederate peace, you cannot have both.

LINCOLN

"If you can look into the seeds of time /
And say which grain will grow and which
will not / Speak then to me . . ."

SEWARD

Oh, disaster. This is a disaster!

LINCOLN

Time is a great thickener of things, Willum.

SEWARD

Yes, I suppose it is.
Actually I have no idea what you mean by
that.

Lincoln stands.

> LINCOLN
> Get me thirteen votes.
> (in a thick Kentucky accent:)
> Them fellers from Richmond ain't here yit.

INT. INSIDE THE AMBULANCE WAGON—DAY

The ambulance has come to a stop. The rear door opens
and the soldiers immediately hop out. The commissioners squint, blinded, into the dazzling sunlight, at the River
Queen, Grant's side-wheel steamer, docked on the banks of
the James River.

TITLE:
U.S. ARMY HEADQUARTERS
CITY POINT, VIRGINIA
JANUARY 12

INT. LINCOLN'S BEDROOM, SECOND FLOOR OF THE
WHITE HOUSE—LATE AFTERNOON

Tad, in fancy military uniform, sits on the bed, Gardner's
box of glass negatives open beside him. He holds up a plate
to a lamp: An old black man with a thick beard and hair,
shirtless.

Tad looks at another plate: A young black woman, head-
scarf, huge ugly scar across her cheek and down her neck.

He studies these with solemn concentration.

> ROBERT (O.C.)
> You drafted half the men in Boston! What
> do you think their families think about me?

Lincoln is being dressed in formal wear by his valet,
WILLIAM SLADE, a light-skinned black man in his forties.
Robert, already in his morning suit, is standing by the door.

> ROBERT
> The only reason they don't throw things
> and spit on me is 'cause you're so popular.
> I can't concentrate on, on British mer-
> cantile law, I don't care about British mer-
> cantile law. I might not even want to be a
> lawyer—

> LINCOLN
> It's a sturdy profession, and a useful one.

> ROBERT
> Yes, and I want to be useful, but *now*, not
> afterwards!

Slade hands Lincoln his formal gloves.

> LINCOLN
> I ain't wearing them things, Mr. Slade, they
> never fit right.

> WILLIAM SLADE
> The missus will have you wear 'em. Don't
> think about leaving 'em.

> ROBERT
> You're delaying, that's your favorite tactic.

WILLIAM SLADE	ROBERT
(to Robert:)	You won't tell me no, but the
Be useful and stop	war will be over in a month,
distracting him.	and you know it will!

LINCOLN
(to Robert:)
I've found that prophesying is one of life's
less prophet-able occupations!

He accepts the gloves. Slade laughs a little, Robert scowls.
Tad holds another glass negative up to the light.

TAD
Why do some slaves cost more than others?

ROBERT
If they're still young and healthy, if the
women can still conceive, they'll pay more—

LINCOLN
Put 'em back in the box. We'll return them
to Mr. Gardner's studio day after next. Be
careful with 'em, now.
(tugging at his gloves:)
These things should've stayed on the calf.

TAD
(to Slade, putting the plates away:)
When you were a slave, Mr. Slade, did they
beat you?

WILLIAM SLADE
I was born a free man. Nobody beat me
except I beat them right back.

There's a knock on the door and Mrs. Keckley enters.

ELIZABETH KECKLEY
Mr. Lincoln, could you come with me—

WILLIAM SLADE
(to Tad:)
Mrs. Keckley was a slave. Ask her if she was
beaten.

	LINCOLN
TAD	(shakes his head:)
Were you—	

Tad.

ELIZABETH KECKLEY
(to Tad:)
I was beaten with a fire shovel when I was
younger than you.
(to Lincoln:)
You should go to Mrs. Lincoln. She's in Willie's room.

ROBERT
She never goes in there.

Lincoln starts toward the door just as John Hay enters,
dressed in the uniform of a Brevet Colonel.

JOHN HAY
The reception line is already stretching out
the door.

Robert shoots an angry, envious glance at Hay's uniform as
Lincoln, Slade, Mrs. Keckley and Hay leave. Robert calls to
his father:

ROBERT
I'll be the only man over fifteen and under
sixty-five in this whole place not in uniform.

TAD
I'm under fifteen and I have a uniform.

Robert storms out.

INT. THE PRINCE OF WALES BEDROOM—AFTERNOON

Lincoln enters a dark room, its heavy drapes closed against
the dim afternoon light. There are two beds. One is stripped
bare. The other is canopied with a thick black veil.

Mary, dressed in a deep purple gown with black flowers
and beading, perfectly pitched between mourning and
emergence, is seated at the head of the canopied bed. On a
nightstand next to the bed there's a toy locomotive engine, a
tattered book of B&O railroad schedules.

Mary holds a framed photograph: an image of WILLIE,
twelve, handsome, bright-eyed, confident.

Lincoln crosses to the window.

> MARY
>
> My head hurts so.
>> (Beat.)
> I prayed for death the night Willie died.
> The headaches are how I know I didn't get
> my wish. How to endure the long afternoon
> and deep into the night.

> LINCOLN
>
> I know.

> MARY
>
> Trying not to think about him. How will
> I manage?

> LINCOLN
>
> Somehow you will.

> MARY
>
>> (sad smile:)
> Somehow. Somehow. Somehow . . . Every
> party, every . . . And now, four years more in

this terrible house reproaching us. He was
a very sick little boy. We should've canceled
that reception, shouldn't we?

LINCOLN
We didn't know how sick he was.

MARY
I knew, I *knew*, I saw that night he was dying.

LINCOLN
Three years ago, the war was going so badly,
and we had to put on a face.

MARY
But I saw Willie was dying. I saw him—

He bends and kisses her hand.

LINCOLN
Molly. It's too hard. Too hard.

Mary stares up at him, her face heavy and swollen with grief.

INT. THE EAST ROOM, WHITE HOUSE—LATE
AFTERNOON

Mary, radiant, her charm turned to its brightest candle-
power, is greeting the Blairs, who are part of a long receiving
line. The Blairs proceed from Mary to Lincoln.

TITLE:
**GRAND RECEPTION
JANUARY 15**

The enormous room is splendid, decked with garlands of
flowers, tall candelabra burning, flags from Army divisions.
An orchestra plays.

Lincoln and Tad stand together. Slade is near Lincoln. Mary's a distance away from Lincoln, to his right.

Robert takes his place next to his mother, as conspicuous as he'd feared he'd be in his civilian clothes.

A sea of people surround the president and his family. Nicolay, Hay and several clerks channel the crowd waiting to greet the Lincolns into the line: wealthy people, many more middle-class people, some working people and farmers, and many officers and soldiers.

Tad watches his father shake hands. Lincoln is in his element. He stands close to each person, touches each one gently, stoops to be nearer them; he puts everyone at ease.

He's bothered only by the white kid gloves he's wearing. He tugs at the right-hand glove.

> WILLIAM SLADE
> (with a glance in Mary's direction:)
> She's just ten feet yonder. I'd like to keep
> my job.

Lincoln takes off the right-hand glove—his hand-shaking hand—but keeps the other glove on.

Approaching Mary on the line, Stevens, Ashley, Senators Bluff Wade and CHARLES SUMNER, all in formal wear except Stevens.

> MARY
> Senator Sumner, it has been much too long.

> CHARLES SUMNER
> "Oh, who can look on that celestial face
> and—"

Cutting him off, she pretends not to recognize Ashley.

> MARY
> And . . . ?

> JAMES ASHLEY
> (confused:)
> James Ashley, ma'am, we've met several
> times—

But she ignores him and greets Stevens.

> MARY
> (her Southern accent becoming more
> lustrous:)
> Praise heavens, praise heavens, just when
> I had abandoned hope of amusement,
> it's the Chairman of the House Ways and
> Means Committee!

Stevens bows to her.

> THADDEUS STEVENS
> Mrs. Lincoln.

> MARY
> Madam President if you please!
> (laughs:)
> Oh, don't convene another subcommittee
> to investigate me, sir! I'm teasing! Smile,
> Senator Wade.

> BLUFF WADE
> (not smiling:)
> I believe I am smiling, Mrs. Lincoln.

> MARY
> I'll take your word for that, sir!

THADDEUS STEVENS
As long as your household accounts are in
order, madam, we'll have no need to inves-
tigate them.

MARY
You have always taken such a lively, even
prosecutorial interest in my household
accounts.

THADDEUS STEVENS
Your household accounts have always been
so interesting.

MARY
Yes, thank you, it's true, the miracles I have
wrought out of fertilizer bills and cutlery
invoices. But I had to! Four years ago, when
the president and I arrived, this was pure
pigsty. Tobacco stains in the turkey carpets.
Mushrooms, green as the moon, sprouting
from ceilings! And a pauper's pittance allot-
ted for improvements. As if your committee
joined with all of Washington awaiting, in
what you anticipated would be our comfort
in squalor, further proof that my husband
and I were prairie primitives, unsuited to
the position to which an error of the people, a flaw in the democratic process, had
elevated us.

Lincoln, suddenly without anyone in line to receive, looks to
see the backlog forming behind the radicals. He notes the
exchange, but says nothing. Robert sees him looking.

MARY
The past is the past, it's a new year now and
we are all getting along, or so they tell me.

I gather we are working together! The White
House and the other House? Hatching little
plans together?

Robert leans in to her.

> ROBERT

Mother?

> MARY

What?

> ROBERT

You're creating a bottleneck.

> MARY

Oh!
> (to Stevens:)
Oh, I'm detaining you, and more important, the people behind you! How the people love my husband, they flock to see him,
by their thousands on public days! They will
never love you the way they love him. How
difficult it must be for you to know that.
And yet how important to remember it.

She gives him a slight, lethal smile. He holds the look; his
poker-face yields to a barely perceptible smile, amused and
perhaps a little admiring.

INT. THE WHITE HOUSE KITCHEN—EVENING

The kitchen's piled with unwashed cookware, eggshells,
flour bins, muffin and pastry molds, spoons and knives, the
detritus of the preparations for the finger food served at the
reception, which has now transitioned into a dance and is
still underway upstairs. Music, the tramp of dancing feet and
rhythmic clapping is audible.

A BLACK FOOTMAN carrying a huge tray laden with dishes and cups comes down the stairs. He hastily beats a retreat when he sees Lincoln and Thaddeus Stevens quietly talking amid the mess.

LINCOLN
Since we have the floor next in the debate,
I thought I'd suggest you might . . . temper
your contributions so as not to frighten our
conservative friends?

THADDEUS STEVENS
Ashley insists you're ensuring approval by
dispensing patronage to otherwise unde-
serving Democrats.

LINCOLN
I can't ensure a single damn thing if you
scare the whole House with talk of land
appropriations and revolutionary tribunals
and punitive thisses and thats—

THADDEUS STEVENS
When the war ends, I intend to push for full
equality, the Negro vote and much more.
Congress shall mandate the seizure of every
foot of rebel land and every dollar of their
property. We'll use their confiscated wealth
to establish hundreds of thousands of free
Negro farmers, and at their side soldiers
armed to occupy and transform the heri-
tage of traitors. We'll build up a land down
there of free men and free women and free
children and freedom. The nation needs to
know that we have such plans.

LINCOLN
That's the untempered version of reconstruction. It's not . . . It's not *exactly* what

I intend, but we shall oppose one another
in the course of time. Now we're working
together, and I'm asking you—

THADDEUS STEVENS
For patience, I expect.

LINCOLN
When the people disagree, bringing them
together requires going slow till they're
ready to make up—

THADDEUS STEVENS
Ah, shit on the people and what they want
and what they're ready for! I don't give a
goddamn about the people and what they
want! This is the face of someone who has
fought long and hard for the good of the
people without caring much for any of 'em.
And I look a lot worse without the wig. The
people elected me! To represent them! To
lead them! And I lead! You ought to try it!

LINCOLN
I admire your zeal, Mr. Stevens, and I have
tried to profit from the example of it.
But if I'd listened to you, I'd've declared
every slave free the minute the first shell
struck Fort Sumter; then the border states
would've gone over to the Confederacy, the
war would've been lost and the Union along
with it, and instead of abolishing slavery, as
we hope to do, in two weeks, we'd be watching helpless as infants as it spread from the
American South into South America.

Stevens glares at him, then smiles.

THADDEUS STEVENS
Oh, how you have longed to say that to me.
You claim you trust them—but you know
what the people are. You know that the
inner compass that should direct the soul
toward justice has ossified in white men and
women, North and South, unto utter use-
lessness through tolerating the evil of slavery. White people cannot bear the thought
of sharing this country's infinite abundance
with Negroes.

Lincoln reaches over to Stevens and gives his shoulder a vig-
orous shake. Stevens endures this.

LINCOLN
A compass, I learnt when I was surveying,
it'll—it'll point you True North from where
you're standing, but it's got no advice about
the swamps and deserts and chasms that
you'll encounter along the way. If in pursuit
of your destination you plunge ahead, heed-
less of obstacles, and achieve nothing more
than to sink in a swamp, what's the use of
knowing True North?

INT. MARY'S BOUDOIR, THE WHITE HOUSE—NIGHT

Spectacles on, Lincoln unlaces Mary's corset.

LINCOLN
Robert's going to plead with us to let him
enlist.

He's unlaced enough; she unhooks the front and steps out
of her corset and petticoats, turns to him in her plain thin
chemise and drawers.

MARY

Make time to talk to Robbie. You only have
time for Tad.

LINCOLN

Tad's young.

MARY

So's Robert. Too young for the Army.

LINCOLN

Plenty of boys younger than Robert signing
up . . .

MARY

Don't take Robbie. Don't let me lose my son.

There's a knock on the door. Mary turns to it, furious:

MARY

Go away! We're occupied!

Lincoln opens the door. Nicolay's standing there.

JOHN NICOLAY

Secretary Stanton has sent me over to tell
you that as of half an hour ago, the shelling
of Wilmington harbor has commenced.

Lincoln leaves with Nicolay. Mary watches, frozen, unable to
let him go, knowing she can't stop him.

INT. THE TELEGRAPH OFFICE, WAR DEPARTMENT—
LATE NIGHT

The telegraph office looks improvised, even after four years.
Formerly the War Department library, it's lined with book-

cases stuffed with bundled dispatches. Telegraph cables stretch across the ceiling to the cipher-operators' desks.

Stanton, perpetually exhausted and impatient, storms down the stairs with Welles and the chief telegraph operator, MAJOR THOMAS ECKERT, forty, in his wake.

> STANTON
> They cannot possibly maintain under this kind of an assault. Terry's got ten thousand men surrounding the goddamned fort! Why doesn't he answer my cables?

WELLES	MAJOR ECKERT
Fort Fisher is a mountain of a building, Edwin. Twenty-two big seacoast guns on each rampart—	It's the largest fort they have, sir. They've been reinforcing it for the last two years—

They reach the desks for the key operators. Among these, SAMUEL BECKWITH, twenty-five, and the key manager, DAVID HOMER BATES, twenty-two, sit at their silent keys, waiting to receive news. Stanton scribbles furiously on Beckwith's small notepad.

> STANTON
> They've taken seventeen thousand shells since yesterday!

WELLES	STANTON
The commander is an old goat.	I want to hear that Fort Fisher's ours and Wilmington has fallen!

> MAJOR ECKERT
> They said—

> STANTON
> Send another damn cable!

Stanton thrusts the cable at Beckwith, who taps it out immediately.

Stanton turns to a table where the large map of Wilmington from the Cabinet meeting is laid out, heavily scribbled-on. GUSTAVUS FOX, assistant Secretary of the Navy, and CHARLES BENJAMIN, Stanton's clerk, are checking the marks on the map against a stack of dispatches.

> STANTON
>
> The problem's their commander Whiting. He engineered the fortress himself. The damned thing's his child; he'll defend it till his every last man is gone. He is not thinking rationally, he's—

> LINCOLN
>
> (hollering:)
> "Come on out, you old rat!"

Everyone's startled, and confused. They all turn to Lincoln, who sits in Major Eckert's chair, wrapped in his shawl.

> LINCOLN
>
> That's what Ethan Allen called to the commander of Fort Ticonderoga in 1776. "Come on out, you old rat!" 'Course there were only forty-odd redcoats at Ticonderoga. But, but there is one Ethan Allen story that I'm very partial to—

> STANTON
>
> No! No, you're, you're going to tell a story! I don't believe that I can bear to listen to another one of your stories right now!

Stanton stalks out, shouting down the corridor as he goes:

> STANTON
>
> I need the B&O sideyard schedules for
> Alexandria! I asked for them this morning!

Lincoln pays no attention to Stanton's fulminations and continues with his story.

> LINCOLN
>
> It was right after the Revolution, right after
> peace had been concluded, and Ethan
> Allen went to London to help our new
> country conduct its business with the king.
> The English sneered at how rough we are,
> and rude and simple-minded and on like
> that, everywhere he went, till one day he
> was invited to the townhouse of a great
> English lord. Dinner was served, beverages
> imbibed, time passed, as happens, and Mr.
> Allen found he needed the privy. He was
> grateful to be directed thence—relieved
> you might say.

Everyone laughs.

> LINCOLN
>
> Now, Mr. Allen discovered on entering
> the water closet that the only decoration
> therein was a portrait of George Washington.
> Ethan Allen done what he came to do and
> returned to the drawing room. His host
> and the others were disappointed when
> he didn't mention Washington's portrait.
> And finally His Lordship couldn't resist,
> and asked Mr. Allen had he noticed it, the
> picture of Washington. He had. Well, what
> did he think of its placement, did it seem
> appropriately located to Mr. Allen? Mr.
> Allen said it did. His host was astounded!

Appropriate? George Washington's likeness
in a water closet? Yes, said Mr. Allen, where
it'll do good service: the whole world knows
nothing'll make an Englishman shit quicker
than the sight of George Washington.

Everyone laughs.

                    LINCOLN
        I love that story.

Beckwith and Bates's keys starts clicking. They transcribe
furiously.

There's a general rush to the operators' desks. Lincoln walks
quickly over, and is joined there by Stanton, who arrives
just as the first dispatch has been completed and is being
decoded. Stanton and Lincoln hold hands, as they've done
many times, waiting for news of the battle.

Bates hands the decoded cable to Benjamin, who reads it
quickly, then announces to the room:

                CHARLES BENJAMIN
        Fort Fisher is ours. We've taken the port.

                    WELLES
        And Wilmington?

Eckert shakes his head as Beckwith hands him the next
telegram.

                  MAJOR ECKERT
        We've taken the fort, but the city of Wil-
        mington has not surrendered.

A beat as this sinks in. Then:

                         STANTON
              How many casualties?

Eckert looks up at Stanton and Lincoln, stricken.

INT. THE HOUSE CHAMBER—DAY

One representative's reading a paper with the headline:
"The Fallen at Wilmington," followed by hundreds of names.

Pendleton and Wood are conferring.

                      FERNANDO WOOD
              Heavy losses.

                    GEORGE PENDLETON
              And more to come.

                      FERNANDO WOOD
              Sours the national mood. That might suf-
              fice to discourage him—

                    GEORGE PENDLETON
              To what? To bring this down? Not in a fight
              like this. This is to the death.

                      FERNANDO WOOD
              It's gruesome!

                    GEORGE PENDLETON
                   (getting upset:)
              Are you despairing, or merely lazy? This
              fight is for *The United States of America*! Noth-
              ing "suffices." A *rumor*? Nothing! *They're* not
              lazy! They're busily buying votes! While we
              hope to be saved by "the national mood"?!

He looks over at Stevens, who's at his desk consulting with
Ashley and Julian.

> GEORGE PENDLETON
> Before this blood is dry, when Stevens next
> takes the floor, taunt him—you excel at
> that—get him to proclaim what we all know
> he believes in his coal-colored heart: that
> this vote is meant to set the black race on
> high, to niggerate America.

> FERNANDO WOOD
> George, please. Stay on course.

> GEORGE PENDLETON
> Bring Stevens to full froth. I can ensure that
> every newspaperman from Louisville to San
> Francisco will be here to witness it and print it.

Colfax gavels the chamber to order, as George Yeaman
approaches the podium.

> SCHUYLER COLFAX
> The floor belongs to the mellifluent gentle-
> man from Kentucky, Mr. George Yeaman.

> GEORGE YEAMAN
> I thank you, Speaker Colfax.

The Democrats applaud as Yeaman takes his place at the
podium and surveys the chamber.

> GEORGE YEAMAN
> Although I'm disgusted by slavery I rise on
> this sad and solemn day to announce that
> I'm opposed to the amendment. We must
> consider what will become of colored folk if
> four million are in one instant set free.

Cheers and boos.

ASA VINTNER LITTON
They'll be free, George! That's what'll
become of them! What'll become of any of
us?! That's what being free means!

Schell, Latham and Bilbo are perched in their usual gallery
seats, taking notes.

RICHARD SCHELL
Think how splendid if Mr. Yeaman switched.

ROBERT LATHAM
(shaking his head:)
Too publicly against us. He can't change
course now.

W. N. BILBO
Not for some miserable little job anyways.

GEORGE YEAMAN
And, and! We will be forced to enfranchise
the men of the colored race—it would be
inhuman not to! Who among us is prepared
to give Negroes the vote?

He's momentarily silenced by cheers and boos throughout
the chamber.

GEORGE YEAMAN
And, and! What shall follow upon that? Uni-
versal enfranchisement? Votes for women?

Yeaman is stopped, baffled and dismayed by the explosion
he's provoked.

INT. AN EMPTY COMMITTEE ROOM, THE CAPITOL—DAY

Hawkins enters and stops when he sees Pendleton and
Wood. It's a trap. LeClerk follows, closing the door.

> FERNANDO WOOD
> Bless my eyes, if it isn't the Postmaster of
> Millersburg Ohio!

Hawkins looks at LeClerk, who guiltily avoids his glance.

> GEORGE PENDLETON
> Mr. LeClerk felt honor-bound to inform us.
> Of your disgusting betrayal. Your prostitution.

> FERNANDO WOOD
> Is that true, Postmaster Hawkins? Is your
> maidenly virtue for sale?

Hawkins sinks.

EXT. A WOODS ALONG THE POTOMAC RIVER—
MORNING

Bilbo and Clay Hawkins are again in the woods. Bilbo, with
his basket, clutches a pair of noisy snared partridges.

> CLAY HAWKINS
> My neighbors hear that I voted yes for nigger
> freedom and no to peace, they will kill me.

> W. N. BILBO
> A deal's a deal and your men know better
> than to piss your pants just 'cause there's
> talk about peace talks.

W. N. BILBO	CLAY HAWKINS
My neighbors in Nashville, they found out I was loyal to the Union, they came after me with gelding knives!	Look, I'll find another job.

Hawkins runs away from Bilbo. Bilbo chases him.

CLAY HAWKINS	W. N. BILBO
(to himself, as he runs:) *Any* other job.	YOU DO RIGHT, CLAY HAWKINS! AND MAKE YOURSELF SOME MONEY IN THE BARGAIN—

CLAY HAWKINS
(turning back to Bilbo:)
I want to do right! *But I got no courage!!!*

Hawkins runs away, sobbing. Bilbo pursues.

W. N. BILBO
Wait!! You wanted, what was it, Tax Man for the Western Reserve, hell you can have the whole state of Ohio if you—

Bilbo stops, winded.

W. N. BILBO
Aw, crap.

EXT. IN A BACK ALLEY, SOMEWHERE IN WASHINGTON—AFTERNOON

Seward, smoking unhappily, strides toward his carriage, with Schell, Latham and Bilbo in pursuit.

SEWARD

Eleven votes?! Two days ago we had twelve!!
What happened?

RICHARD SCHELL

It's the goddamned rumors
regarding the Richmond
delegation.

ROBERT LATHAM

There are defections in the
ranks—
Yes! The peace offer!

SEWARD

Groundless. I told you that.

ROBERT LATHAM

And yet the rumors persist.

RICHARD SCHELL

They are ruining us.
Among the few remaining representatives
who seem remotely plausible there is a perceptible increase in resistance.

Seward has reached the carriage, Bilbo alongside him.
Before the Secretary of State can climb on board, Bilbo
shuts the carriage door. Seward is outraged.

W. N. BILBO

Resistance, hell! Thingamabob Hollister,
Dem from Indiana? I approached him, the
sumbitch near to murdered me!

EXT. A STREET IN GEORGETOWN—NIGHT

Bilbo is talking to HAROLD HOLLISTER (D, IN), who pulls
out a derringer. Bilbo bolts, dropping the folder. He stops,
runs back, and bends to retrieve the folio as Hollister fires
the gun over Bilbo's head.

EXT. IN A BACK ALLEY, SOMEWHERE IN WASHINGTON—
AFTERNOON

Seward, now inside the carriage, slams the door.

SEWARD
Perhaps you push too hard.

W. N. BILBO
I push nobody. Perhaps we need reinforce-
ments. If Jeff Davis wants to cease hostilities,
who do you think'll give a genuine solid shit
to free slaves?

SEWARD
Get back to it, and good day, gentlemen.

Schell and Latham lean in to the carriage.

RICHARD SCHELL
We are at an impasse.

ROBERT LATHAM
Tell Lincoln to deny the rumors. Publicly.

RICHARD SCHELL
Tell us what you expect of us.

SEWARD
I expect you to do your work! And to have
sufficient sense and taste not to presume to
instruct the president. Or me.

Schell steps up on the running board, intent.

RICHARD SCHELL
Is there a Confederate offer or not?

EXT. THE JAMES RIVER DOCK AT CITY POINT,
VIRGINIA—DAY

ULYSSES S. GRANT, forty-three, 5'7", beard, uniform worn
and rumpled, crosses the dock, followed by three aides.

They approach the gangway for the River Queen.

INT. THE RIVER QUEEN SALOON, CITY POINT,
VIRGINIA—DAY

Grant and the commissioners stand in an expansive cabin at
the stern, patriotically decorated, large windows.

Grant hands the commissioners' peace proposal back to
them. He's scribbled notes all over the document.

> GRANT
> I suggest you work some changes to your
> proposal before you give it to the president.

> R. M. T. HUNTER
> We're eager to be on our way to Washington.

> ALEXANDER STEPHENS
> Did Mr. Lincoln tell you to tell us this, Gen-
> eral Grant?

Grant fixes Stephens with a look—bemused, a little disap-
pointed.

> GRANT
> It says ". . . securing peace for our two coun-
> tries." And it goes on like that.

> ALEXANDER STEPHENS
> I don't know what you—

GRANT

There's just one country. You and I, we're citizens of that country. I'm fighting to protect it from armed rebels. From you.

ALEXANDER STEPHENS

But Mr. Blair told us, he, he told President Davis we were—

GRANT

A private citizen like Preston Blair can say what he pleases, since he has no authority over anything. If you want to discuss peace with President Lincoln, consider revisions.

He lights a cigar.

ALEXANDER STEPHENS

If we're not to discuss a truce between warring nations, what in Heaven's name can we discuss?

GRANT

Terms of surrender.

EXT. THE JAMES RIVER DOCK AT CITY POINT, VIRGINIA—DAY

As a somber Grant disembarks with his aides from the River Queen:

GRANT

"Office United States Military Telegraph, War Department for Abraham Lincoln, President of the United States. January 20, 1865. I will state confidentially that I am convinced, upon conversation with these

commissioners, that their intentions are
good and their desire sincere to restore
peace and union. I fear now their going
back, without any expression of interest . . ."

Seward's voice takes over from Grant's.

GRANT	SEWARD (V.O.)
". . . from anyone in authority, Mr. Lincoln . . ."	". . . from anyone in authority, Mr. Lincoln . . ."

INT. SEWARD MANSION, LAFAYETTE SQUARE,
WASHINGTON—NIGHT

Seward's in a fancy robe and slippers, reading a telegram.

                    SEWARD
". . . will have a bad influence.
I will be sorry should it prove impossible
for you to have an interview with them.
I am awaiting your instructions. U. S. Grant,
Lieutenant General Commanding Armies
United States."

Lincoln is in his coat, shawl over his shoulders, holding his hat.

                    LINCOLN
After four years of war and near six hundred thousand lives lost. He believes we can
end this war now.
My trust in him is marrow deep.

Seward looks up at Lincoln, then down again at the telegram. He stands and crosses to Lincoln.

                    SEWARD
You could bring the delegates to Washington. In exchange for the South's immedi-

ate surrender, we could promise them the
amendment's defeat. They'd agree, don't
you think? We'd end the war. This week.

Lincoln has closed his eyes.

> SEWARD
> Or. If you could manage, without seeming
> to do it, to—

Lincoln shakes his head no.

> SEWARD
> The peace delegation might encounter
> delays as they travel up the James River. Par-
> ticularly with the fighting around
> Wilmington.
> Within ten days time, we might pass the
> Thirteenth Amendment.

INT. HALLWAY, THE WHITE HOUSE—LATE NIGHT

Lincoln, shawl still wrapped around him, walks the long
empty hall.

INT. LINCOLN'S OFFICE, WHITE HOUSE—LATE NIGHT

Lincoln sits before an open window. He's disheveled, in
shirtsleeves an unbuttoned vest, next to an inkwell, papers
and books of law scattered about, and a lit candle in a can-
dlestick, guttering. Grant's telegraph is in one hand, and in
the other hand, his spectacles and, dangling from a chain,
his open pocket watch. His bare left foot keeps time with the
watch's loud ticking. He stares out into the cold night.

INT. JOHN HAY AND JOHN NICOLAY'S BEDROOM—
EVEN LATER

The room is spare and neat. Nicolay and Hay are asleep in
their beds.

Lincoln is sitting at the foot of Hay's bed, spectacles on,
reading a petition, the others in his lap, pencil in hand.

> LINCOLN
> Now, here's a sixteen-year-old boy. They're
> going to hang him . . .

Hay startles awake, then settles. He's used to this.

> LINCOLN
> (he reads a little further:)
> He was with the 15th Indiana Calvary near
> Beaufort, seems he lamed his horse to avoid
> battle. I don't think even Stanton would
> complain if I pardoned him. You think
> Stanton would complain?

Nicolay stirs in the next bed.

> JOHN HAY
> Ummm . . . I don't know, sir, I don't know
> who you're, uh . . . What time is it?

> LINCOLN
> It's three-forty in the morning.

> JOHN NICOLAY
> (not waking up:)
> Don't . . . let him pardon any more desert-
> ers . . .

Nicolay's asleep again.

JOHN HAY
Mr. Stanton thinks you pardon too many.
He's generally apoplectic on the subject—

LINCOLN
He oughtn't to have done that, crippled
his horse, that was cruel, but you don't just
hang a sixteen-year-old boy for that—

JOHN HAY
Ask the horse what he thinks.

LINCOLN
—for cruelty. There'd be no sixteen-year-
old boys left.
    (a beat, then:)
Grant wants me to bring the secesh delegates to Washington.

JOHN HAY
So . . . There *are* secesh delegates?

LINCOLN
    (scribbling a note, signing the petition:)
He was afraid, that's all it was. I don't care
to hang a boy for being frightened, either.
What good would it do him?

He signs the pardon. Then he gives Hay's leg a few hard
thwacks and a squeeze. It hurts a little. Hay winces.

LINCOLN
War's nearly done. Ain't that so?
What use one more corpse? Any more
corpses?

Putting the rest of the petitions on Hay's bed, he stands to
leave.

JOHN HAY
Do you need company?

INT. HALLWAY, THE WHITE HOUSE—LATE NIGHT

As before, Lincoln continues his slow and solitary walk.

LINCOLN (V.O.)
Times like this, I'm best alone.

INT. THE TELEGRAPH ROOM, WAR DEPARTMENT—
PRE-DAWN

Lincoln is seated at Eckert's desk, shawl wrapped around
his shoulders, glasses on; he stares down into his hat, held
between his knees. David Homer Bates and Samuel Beckwith
are waiting for him.

Lincoln draws a handwritten note from his hat and carefully
unfolds it.

LINCOLN
"Lieutenant General Ulysses S. Grant, City
Point. I have read your words with interest."

Sam Beckwith transcribes Lincoln's words into code on a
pad with a pencil.

LINCOLN
"I ask that, regardless of any action I take
in the matter of the visit of the Richmond
commissioners, you maintain among your
troops military preparedness for battle, as
you have done until now."

He stops for a moment. Beckwith waits, pencil poised.

Lincoln looks at the note, folds it, tucks it in a band inside his hat.

LINCOLN
"Have Captain Saunders convey the com-
missioners to me here in Washington."
(Another pause.)
"A. Lincoln." And the date.

SAMUEL BECKWITH
(while writing:)
Yes, sir.

Lincoln places the hat on the floor.

SAMUEL BECKWITH
Shall I transmit, sir?

LINCOLN
(a beat, then:)
You think we choose to be born?

SAMUEL BECKWITH
I don't suppose so.

LINCOLN
Are we fitted to the times we're born into?

SAMUEL BECKWITH
I don't know about myself. You may be, sir.
Fitted.

LINCOLN
(to Homer:)
What do you reckon?

DAVID HOMER BATES
I'm an engineer. I reckon there's machinery
but no one's done the fitting.

LINCOLN
You're an engineer, you must know Euclid's
axioms and common notions.

DAVID HOMER BATES
I must've in school, but . . .

LINCOLN
I never had much of schooling, but I read
Euclid, in an old book I borrowed. Little
enough ever found its way in here—
    (touching his cranium:)
—but once learnt it stayed learnt.
Euclid's first common notion is this:
"Things which are equal to the same thing
are equal to each other."

David doesn't get it; neither does Sam.

LINCOLN
That's a rule of mathematical reasoning. It's
true because it works; has done and always
will do. In his book, Euclid says this is "self-
evident."
    (Beat.)
D'you see? There it is, even in that two-
thousand-year-old book of mechanical law:
it is a self-evident truth that things which
are equal to the same thing are equal to
each other. We begin with equality. That's
the origin, isn't it? That balance—that's fairness, that's justice.

He looks at his scribbled note, then at Sam and Homer.

LINCOLN
Read me the last sentence of my telegram.

SAMUEL BECKWITH
"Have Captain Saunders convey the commissioners to me here in Washington."

LINCOLN
A slight emendation, Sam, if you would.

Beckwith writes as Lincoln dictates.

LINCOLN
"Have Captain Saunders convey the gentlemen aboard the River Queen as far as
Hampton Roads, Virginia, and there wait
until . . ."
(Beat.)
". . . further advice from me. Do not proceed to Washington."

INT. HOUSE CHAMBER, THE CAPITOL—LATE MORNING

The chamber's noisy and packed. In the balcony's front row,
a wall of newspapermen, notebooks at the ready.

TITLE:
**HOUSE OF REPRESENTATIVES
JANUARY 27**

Ashley, Colfax and Stevens approach Stevens's desk. Colfax
nods toward the journalists in the balcony:

SCHUYLER COLFAX
The *World*, the *Herald* and the *Times*, New
York, Chicago, the *Journal of Commerce*, even
your hometown paper's here.

President Abraham Lincoln (Daniel Day-Lewis) surveys the aftermath of the Siege of Petersburg.

(Photos by David James)

Above: Lincoln (Daniel Day-Lewis) has an encounter with Corporal Ira Clark (David Oyelowo) as Clark's cavalry unit prepares for the assault on Wilmington.

Below: Lincoln (Daniel Day-Lewis) meets with his Cabinet to discuss the planned attack on Fort Fisher.

Above: (back row) Robert Todd Lincoln (Joseph Gordon-Levitt), Thomas "Tad" Lincoln (Gulliver McGrath), valet William Slade (Stephen McKinley Henderson) and Abraham Lincoln (Daniel Day-Lewis); (front row) Mary Todd Lincoln (Sally Field), Senator Bluff Wade (Wayne Duvall), Representative Thaddeus Stevens (Tommy Lee Jones), Senator Charles Sumner (John Hutton) and Representative James Ashley (David Costabile) at a White House reception.

Below: Lincoln (Daniel Day-Lewis) with his son Tad (Gulliver McGrath).

Above: Democratic Representative Fernando Wood (Lee Pace) opens the House debate on the Thirteenth Amendment to the Constitution.

Below: Representative Thaddeus Stevens (Tommy Lee Jones) takes the podium during the House debate on the Thirteenth Amendment.

Above: Lincoln (Daniel Day-Lewis) and Lieutenant General Ulysses S. Grant (Jared Harris) discuss the inevitability of Lee's surrender.

Below: Elizabeth Keckley (Gloria Reuben), Mary Todd Lincoln (Sally Field) and Abraham Lincoln (Daniel Day-Lewis) attend a performance of Gounod's *Faust.*

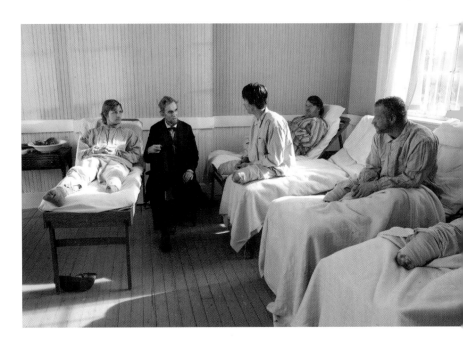

Above: Lincoln (Daniel Day-Lewis) visits wounded soldiers at an army hospital.

Below: On March 4, 1865, Abraham Lincoln (Daniel Day-Lewis) delivers his Second Inaugural Address.

JAMES ASHLEY
(to Stevens:)
Say you believe only in legal equality for
all races, not racial equality, I beg you, sir.
Compromise. Or you risk it all.

Stevens sees Mary, with Mrs. Keckley, claiming front seats
from two journalists.

INT. HOUSE CHAMBER, THE CAPITOL—LATER

Stevens, at the podium, is being challenged by Fernando
Wood, standing at his desk.

FERNANDO WOOD
I've asked you a question, Mr. Stevens, and
you must answer me. Do you or do you not
hold that the precept that "all men are created equal" is meant literally?

All eyes are on Stevens, the chamber quiet except for a
scratching sound: the journalists have begun scribbling.

FERNANDO WOOD
Is that not the true purpose of the amendment? To promote your ultimate and
ardent dream to elevate—

THADDEUS STEVENS
The true purpose of the amendment,
Mr. *Wood*, you perfectly named, brainless,
obstructive *object*?

FERNANDO WOOD
You have always insisted, Mr. Stevens, that
Negroes are the same as white men are.

THADDEUS STEVENS
The true purpose of the amendment—

Stevens looks up at the balcony, at the waiting journalists, and Mary, who raises her eyebrows, then at Ashley and Litton at their desks. Seward watches from the balcony.

Stevens returns to Wood.

THADDEUS STEVENS
I don't hold with equality in all things only with equality before the law and nothing more.

FERNANDO WOOD
(surprised:)
That's not so! You believe that Negroes are entirely equal to white men. You've said it a thousand times—

GEORGE PENDLETON
(leaping to his feet:)
For shame! For shame! Stop prevaricating and answer Representative Wood!

THADDEUS STEVENS	GEORGE PENDLETON
I don't hold with equality in all things, only with equality before the law and nothing more.	(stands:) After the decades of fervent advocacy on behalf of the colored race—

JAMES ASHLEY
(leaping up:)
He's answered your questions! This amendment has naught to do with race equality!

Pendleton persists, through cheers and catcalls.

GEORGE PENDLETON	THADDEUS STEVENS
You have long insisted, have you not, that the dusk-colored race is no different from the white one.	I don't hold with equality in all things only with equality before the law and nothing more.

Among the amendment's supporters, including Litton, a GROUP OF WOMEN SUFFRAGISTS in the balcony, and Elizabeth Keckley, there's visible, audible shock and dismay at Stevens's capitulation. Mary's surprised by Stevens, and impressed.

MARY
(whispering to Mrs. Keckley:)
Who'd ever've guessed that old nightmare capable of such control? He might make a politician some day—

ELIZABETH KECKLEY
(standing abruptly:)
I need to go.

Mary's startled. Mrs. Keckley leaves the balcony, pushing past journalists. On the floor:

GEORGE PENDLETON
Your frantic attempt to delude us now is unworthy of a representative. It is, in fact, unworthy of a white man!

THADDEUS STEVENS
(giving in to his anger:)
How *can* I hold that all men are created equal, when here before me—
(pointing to Pendleton:)
—stands stinking the moral carcass of the gentleman from Ohio, proof that some men *are* inferior, endowed by their Maker

103

with dim wits impermeable to reason with
cold pallid slime in their veins instead of
hot red blood! You are more reptile than
man, George, so low and flat that the foot
of man is incapable of crushing you!

General uproar.

GEORGE PENDLETON
HOW DARE YOU!

THADDEUS STEVENS
Yet even you, Pendleton, who should have
been gibbetted for treason long before
today, even worthless unworthy you ought
to be treated equally before the law! And so
again, sir, and again and again and again
I say: I DO NOT HOLD WITH EQUALITY
IN ALL THINGS. ONLY WITH EQUALITY
BEFORE THE LAW.

Ashley sits, nearly weeping with relief, while the chamber
explodes: laughter, applause, boos.

GEORGE PENDLETON
MR. SPEAKER, WILL YOU PERMIT THIS
VILE BOORISH MAN TO SLANDER AND
TO THREATEN ME?

The journalists pack up their notebooks; this is fun, but not
newsworthy, and only a few bother to record it.

Stevens limps out through the aisle to wild Republican
applause. He looks up to the balcony; Mary is looking down
approvingly. He looks down before she can see him smile.

INT. A CORRIDOR OUTSIDE THE HOUSE CHAMBER—
LATER

Stevens sits on a bench, alone, thinking, troubled. Asa Vintner Litton approaches him.

> ASA VINTNER LITTON
> You asked if ever I was surprised.

Stevens nods.

> ASA VINTNER LITTON
> Today, Mr. Stevens, I was surprised. You've
> led the battle for race equality for thirty
> years! The basis of, of every hope for this
> country's future life, *you denied Negro equal-
> ity*! I'm nauseated. You refused to say that
> all humans are, well . . . human! Have you
> lost your very soul, Mr. Stevens? Is there
> *nothing* you won't say?

Stevens nods, then, quietly:

> THADDEUS STEVENS
> I'm sorry you're nauseous, Asa, that must be
> unpleasant.
> I want the amendment to pass. So that the
> Constitution's first and only mention of
> slavery is its absolute prohibition. For this
> amendment, for which I have worked all
> of my life and for which countless colored
> men and women have fought and died and
> now hundreds of thousands of soldiers—
> no, sir, no, it seems there is very nearly
> nothing I won't say.

EXT. THE STREETS OF WASHINGTON—MORNING

Lincoln and Robert are in the buggy driven by an OLD
SOLDIER; a YOUNG BODYGUARD SOLDIER sits beside
the driver, his rifle uselessly tucked under his legs. Lincoln is
on one side reading over a stack of documents. Robert's on
the other side of the buggy, staring sullenly at his feet.

The buggy stops outside an Army hospital. Lincoln packs up
his papers.

> ROBERT
>
> I'm not going in.

> LINCOLN
>
> You said you wanted to help me.

> ROBERT
>
> This is—this is just a clumsy attempt at dis-
> couragement. I've been to Army hospitals,
> I've seen surgeries, I went and visited the
> malaria barges with Mama.

> LINCOLN
>
> She told me she didn't take you inside.

> ROBERT
>
> I snuck in after—I've seen what it's like.
> This changes nothing.

> LINCOLN
>
> At all rates, I'm happy to have your company.

Stepping out of the buggy, he hands his folio to the bodyguard and enters the Army hospital.

INT. ARMY HOSPITAL—MORNING

Lincoln is met in the antechamber by an ARMY SURGEON.

> LINCOLN
> Morning, Jim.

> ARMY SURGEON
> Hello, Mr. President.

> LINCOLN
> Good to see you again.

They move into the main ward, Lincoln removing his hat.

> LINCOLN
> Well, boys, first question: You getting
> enough to eat?

He walks from bed to bed, shaking hands with each patient.
Most are amputees.

> FIRST PATIENT
> Hello, sir.

> LINCOLN
> What's your name, soldier?

> FIRST PATIENT
> Robert.

> LINCOLN
> Robert. Good to meet you, Robert.

> SECOND PATIENT
> Nice to meet you.

> LINCOLN
> What's your name?

SECOND PATIENT

Kevin.

LINCOLN

Tell me your names as I go past. I like to
know who I'm talkin' to. Kevin.

THIRD PATIENT

Mr. President. John.

LINCOLN

John. I've seen you before.

FOURTH PATIENT

Mr. President . . .

EXT. OUTSIDE THE ARMY HOSPITAL—MORNING

Robert, brooding, waits in the buggy.

Hearing a creaking, rumbling sound, Robert turns to see
TWO BLACK ORDERLIES in gray uniforms wrangling a
large top-heavy wheelbarrow, covered with filthy canvas. One
orderly pushes while the other keeps the barrow from tip-
ping over.

Robert notices, in the barrow's wake, a trail of blood. He
gets out of the buggy and follows as the orderlies turn a corner of the building.

Behind the building, where the ground is bare, pitted with
puddles of water, Robert watches as the orderlies reach the
edge of a shallow pit. One orderly pulls the canvas back,
revealing severed legs, arms, hands, rotten, burnt, shattered
by bullet or bomb.

Robert watches as they toss the remains into the pit. Quick-
lime is shoveled atop the limbs.

Robert walks away, unsteady.

Around the corner, he fumbles through his pockets for rolling paper and tobacco. He locates these and tries to focus on rolling a cigarette, his hands shaking. He tries harder to control his hands, his feelings, but he can't. He has a panic attack, crying, hiccupy shallow breathing, face flushed. Frustrated, he throws down the cigarette and tries to hold back tears.

> LINCOLN (O.C.)
> What's the matter, Bob?

Robert looks up, mortified, to see Lincoln watching him with concern. He wipes his eyes, his mouth.

> ROBERT
> I have to do this! And I will do it and I don't
> need your permission to enlist.

> LINCOLN
> That same speech has been made by how
> many sons to how many fathers since the
> war began? "I don't need your damn per-
> mission, you miserable old goat, I'm gonna
> enlist anyhow!" And what wouldn't those
> numberless fathers have given to be able
> to say to their sons—as I now say to mine—
> "I'm commander-in-chief, so in point of
> fact, without my permission, you ain't enlist-
> ing in nothing, nowhere, young man."

> ROBERT
> It's Mama you're scared of, not me getting
> killed.

Lincoln slaps Robert in the face. It shocks them both.

Lincoln tries to embrace Robert, but Robert shoulders past him and walks back toward the front of he building. He turns.

ROBERT

I have to do this! And I will! Or I will feel
ashamed of myself for the rest of my life.
Whether or not you fought is what's gonna
matter. And not just to other people, but to
myself.
I won't be you, Pa. I can't do that. But
I don't want to be nothing.

He hurries away.

LINCOLN

We can't lose you.

INT. MARY'S BOUDOIR, SECOND FLOOR OF THE
WHITE HOUSE—NIGHT

Outside, driving rain and wind. Lincoln sits by the window,
in his coat, vest and tie, hair combed neatly.

LINCOLN

He'll be fine, Molly. City Point's far from
the front lines, from the fighting, he'll be
an adjutant running messages for General
Grant.

Mary sits at her vanity in a beautiful evening dress, pale with
rage.

MARY

The war will take our son! A sniper, or a
shrapnel shell! Or typhus, same as took Willie, it takes hundreds of boys a day! He'll
die, uselessly, and how will I ever forgive
you? Most men, their firstborn is their favor-
ite, but you, you've always blamed Robert
for being born, for trapping you in a mar-

riage that's only ever given you grief and
caused you regret!

LINCOLN

That's not true—

MARY

And if the slaughter of Cold Harbor is on
your hands same as Grant, God help us!
We'll pay for the oceans of spilled blood
you've sanctioned, the uncountable corpses
we'll be made to pay with our son's dear
blood—

Lincoln rises from the window seat, angry.

LINCOLN

Just, just this once, Mrs. Lincoln, I demand
of you to try and take the liberal and not
the selfish point of view! You imagine Robert will forgive us if we continue to stifle his
very natural ambition?!

MARY
(with a mocking smile:)
And if I refuse to take the high road, if
I won't take up the rough old cross, will you
threaten me again with the madhouse, as
you did when I couldn't stop crying over
Willie, when I showed you what heartbreak,
real heartbreak looked like, and you hadn't
the courage to countenance it, to help
me—

LINCOLN	MARY
That's right. When you	*I* was in the room with
refused so much as to	Willie, I was holding him in
comfort Tad—	my arms as he died!

LINCOLN	MARY
—the child who was not only sick, dangerously sick, but beside himself with grief?	How dare you!

LINCOLN	MARY
Oh but *your* grief, *your* grief, your inexhaustible grief!	How dare you throw that at me?!

LINCOLN	MARY
And his mother won't let him near her, 'cause she's screaming from morning to night pacing the corridors, *howling at shadows and furniture and ghosts*! I ought to have done it, I ought have done for Tad's sake, for *everybody's god-damned sake*, I should have clapped you in the madhouse!	I couldn't let Tad in! I couldn't risk him seeing how *angry I was*!

MARY

THEN DO IT! Do it! Don't you threaten
me, you do it this time! Lock me away!
You'll have to, I swear, if Robert is killed!

Silence. Then:

LINCOLN

I couldn't tolerate you grieving so for Willie because I couldn't permit it in myself,
though I wanted to, Mary. I wanted to crawl
under the earth, into the vault with his cof-
fin. I still do. Every day I do.
Don't . . . talk to me about grief.
    (Beat.)
I must make my decisions, Bob must make
his, you yours. And bear what we must, hold

and carry what we must. What I carry within
me—you must allow me to do it, alone as
I must. And you alone, Mary, you alone may
lighten this burden, or render it intoler-
able. As you choose.

She opens her mouth to make an angry reply, then stops,
and watches as he leaves the room.

INT. ODD FELLOWS' HALL, WASHINGTON—NIGHT

Onstage, Gounod's *Faust*, Act Three, scene eight, the garden
outside Marguerite's cottage, a gorgeously romantic night.
MARGUERITE and FAUST are alone singing. The Lincolns,
in their box, watch quietly. Elizabeth Keckley sits next to Mary.

Mary turns to Lincoln. They speak in whispers. Mrs. Keckley
tries not to listen but she can't help hearing what they say.

                    MARY
        You think I'm ignorant of what you're up to
        because you haven't discussed this scheme
        with me as you ought to have done. When
        have I ever been so easily bamboozled?
            (Beat.)
        I believe you when you insist that amending
        the Constitution and abolishing slavery will
        end this war. And since you are sending my
        son into the war, woe unto you if you fail to
        pass the amendment.

                    LINCOLN
        Seward doesn't want me leaving big muddy
        footprints all over town.

                    MARY
        No one ever lived who knows better than you
        the proper placement of footfalls on treach-

erous paths. Seward can't do it. You must.
Because if you fail to secure the necessary
votes, woe unto you, sir. You will answer to me.

EXT. THE PORTICO OF THE WHITE HOUSE—A SHORT
WHILE LATER

The carriage has pulled up and Mary is entering the White
House. Lincoln helps Mrs. Keckley down from the carriage.

She hesitates before proceeding in. Then she faces Lincoln.

> ELIZABETH KECKLEY
> I know the vote is only four days away;
> I know you're concerned. Thank you for
> your concern over this, and I want you to
> know: They'll approve it. God will see to it.

> LINCOLN
> I don't envy him his task. He may wish He'd
> chosen an instrument for His purpose more
> wieldy than the House of Representatives.

> ELIZABETH KECKLEY
> Then *you'll* see to it.

Lincoln looks at her, considering. Then:

> LINCOLN
> Are you afraid of what lies ahead? For your
> people? If we succeed?

> ELIZABETH KECKLEY
> White people don't want us here.

> LINCOLN
> Many don't.

ELIZABETH KECKLEY
What about you?

LINCOLN
I . . . I don't know you, Mrs. Keckley. Any of
you. You're . . . familiar to me, as all people
are. Unaccommodated, poor, bare, forked
creatures such as we all are. You have a
right to expect what I expect, and likely our
expectations are not incomprehensible to
each other. I assume I'll get used to you.
But what you are to the nation, what'll
become of you once slavery's day is done,
I don't know.

ELIZABETH KECKLEY
What my people are to be, I can't say.
Negroes have been fighting and dying for
freedom since the first of us was a slave.
I never heard any ask what freedom will
bring. Freedom's first. As for me: My son
died, fighting for the Union, wearing the
Union blue. For freedom he died. I'm his
mother. That's what I am to the nation, Mr.
Lincoln. What else must I be?

INT. A BEDROOM IN THE ST. CHARLES HOTEL—LATE
NIGHT

The room is far filthier and more cluttered than before.
Bilbo and Latham are playing cards. Schell is asleep in bed.

W. N. BILBO
My whole hand's gonna be proud in about
five seconds, let's see how proud you gonna
be.

ROBERT LATHAM
Oh, it is? What you got goin'?

There's a quick knock on the door.

W. N. BILBO
Yeah?

ROBERT LATHAM
Go away!
(to Bilbo:)
That watch fob, is that gold?

W. N. BILBO
You keep your eyes off my fob!

Seward enters, displeased, as they show their cards, laughing.

ROBERT LATHAM
Nines paired!

W. N. BILBO
Oh my goddamn!

SEWARD
Gentlemen. You have a visitor.

Latham jovially collects his winnings. He stops short when Lincoln steps into the room, cloak and stovepipe, very tall.

W. N. BILBO
Well, I'll be fucked.

LINCOLN
I wouldn't bet against it, Mr. . . . ?

Schell startles awake as Bilbo puts down his cigar and wipes his hand on his vest.

W. N. BILBO

W. N. Bilbo.

LINCOLN

Mr. Bilbo. Gentlemen.

ROBERT LATHAM

Sir . . .

W. N. BILBO

Why are you here? No offense, but Mr.
Seward's banished the very mention of your
name, he won't even let us use fifty-cent
pieces 'cause they got your face on 'em.

LINCOLN

The Secretary of State here tells me that,
uh, you got eleven Democrats in the bag.
That's encouraging.

ROBERT LATHAM

Oh, you've got no cause to be encouraged.
Sir. Uh . . .

RICHARD SCHELL

Are we being . . . fired?

Lincoln sits at the card table.

LINCOLN

"We have heard the chimes of midnight,
Master Shallow." I'm here to alert you boys
that the great day of reckoning is nigh upon
us.

RICHARD SCHELL

The Democrats we've yet to bag, sir. The
patronage jobs simply won't bag 'em. They
require more . . . convincing, Mr. President.

Lincoln nods. He turns to Bilbo.

> LINCOLN
> Mm-hmm. Do me a favor, willya?

> W. N. BILBO
> Sure.

> LINCOLN
> Snagged my eye in the paper this morning.
> Governor Curtin is set to declare a winner
> in the disputed Congressional election for
> the—

> W. N. BILBO
> Pennsylvania 16th District.

> LINCOLN
> What a joy to be comprehended. Hop on a
> train to Phildell, call on the governor—

> SEWARD
> (looking askance at Bilbo's appearance:)
> Send Latham. Or Schell.

> LINCOLN
> (to Bilbo:)
> No, he'll do fine, just polish yourself up first.

Bilbo, cigar back in mouth, laughs.

> ROBERT LATHAM
> The incumbent is claiming he won it. Name
> of, uh . . .

> W. N. BILBO
> Coffroth.

LINCOLN
That's him.

RICHARD SCHELL
Coffroth. He is a Democrat.

LINCOLN
I understand he is.
Let Governor Curtin know it'd be
much appreciated if he'd invite
the House of Representatives to
decide who won. He's entitled to
do that. He'll agree to it.
    (to Schell:)
Then advise Coffroth, if he hopes to
retain his seat, that he'd better pay
a visit to Thaddeus Stevens.

W. N. BILBO
Silly name.

SEWARD
Pity poor Coffroth.

INT. THADDEUS STEVENS'S OFFICE, THE CAPITOL—
NIGHT

Stevens is at his desk, paperwork piled high. There's a knock
at the door.

THADDEUS STEVENS
It opens!

A nervous man enters hesitantly: Alexander Coffroth.

Stevens glares at him with what looks like horror. Coffroth's
frightened smile transforms into a rictus of pain. Then:

THADDEUS STEVENS
You are Canfrey?

ALEXANDER COFFROTH
Coffroth, Mr. Stevens, Alexander Coffroth,
I'm, I'm—

THADDEUS STEVENS
(skeptical:)
Are we representatives of the same state?

ALEXANDER COFFROTH
Y-yes sir! We sit only three desks apart—

Stevens waves him into a chair.

THADDEUS STEVENS
I haven't noticed you. I'm a Republican,
and *you*, Coughdrop, are a Democrat?

ALEXANDER COFFROTH
Well, I . . . Um, that is to say . . . I—

THADDEUS STEVENS
The modern travesty of Thomas Jefferson's
political organization to which you have
attached yourself like a barnacle has the
effrontery to call itself The Democratic
Party. You are a Dem-o-crat.
What's the matter with you? Are you
wicked?

ALEXANDER COFFROTH
Well, I felt, um, formerly, I—

THADDEUS STEVENS
Never mind, Coffsnot. You were ignomini-
ously trounced at the hustings in Novem-
ber's election by your worthy challenger, a
Republican—

ALEXANDER COFFROTH
No, sir, I was not, um, trounced! Uh, he wants
to steal my seat! I didn't lose the election—

THADDEUS STEVENS
What difference does it make if you lost or
not?! The governor of our state, is . . . ? A
Democrat?

ALEXANDER COFFROTH
No, he's a . . .
        (baffled, terrified:)
A, um, a Ruh . . .

THADDEUS STEVENS
Re.

ALEXANDER COFFROTH
Re.

THADDEUS STEVENS
        (nods:)
Pub.

ALEXANDER COFFROTH
Pub.

THADDEUS STEVENS
Li.

ALEXANDER COFFROTH
Li.

THADDEUS STEVENS
Can.

ALEXANDER COFFROTH
Can.
Republican.

THADDEUS STEVENS
I know what he is. This is a rhetorical exer-
cise. And Congress is controlled by what
party? Yours?

Coffroth doesn't know whether to answer. He shakes his head.

THADDEUS STEVENS
Your party was *beaten*, your challenger's
party now controls the House, and hence
the House Committee on Elections, so *you*
have been *beaten*. You shall shortly be sent
home in disgrace. Unless.

ALEXANDER COFFROTH
I know what I must do, sir! I will immediately
become a Republican and vote yes for—

THADDEUS STEVENS
NO! *Coffroth* will vote yes but *Coffroth* will
remain a Democrat until after he does so.

ALEXANDER COFFROTH
Why wait to switch? I'm happy to switch—

THADDEUS STEVENS
We want to show the amendment has bipar-
tisan support, you idiot.
Early in the next Congress, when I tell you
to do so, you will switch parties. Now congratulations on your victory, and get out.

INT. A BEDROOM IN THE ST. CHARLES HOTEL—LATE
NIGHT

Lincoln and his operatives around the card table.

LINCOLN
Now give me the names of whoever else you
been hunting.

Schell, Latham and Bilbo exchange looks, then:

ROBERT LATHAM
George Yeaman.

RICHARD SCHELL
Yes. Yeaman.

W. N. BILBO
Among others. But Yeaman: That'd count.

ROBERT LATHAM
(helpfully:)
Y-E-A-M-A-N.

Lincoln looks up from his notepad, smiling.

LINCOLN
I got it.

ROBERT LATHAM
Kentucky.

INT. SEWARD'S OFFICE, STATE DEPARTMENT—DAY

Seward sits at his grand desk, looking on with an anxious
scowl. Lincoln sits on the edge of Seward's desk. Yeaman sits
in a chair facing him.

GEORGE YEAMAN
I can't vote for the amendment, Mr. Lincoln.

LINCOLN

I saw a barge once, Mr. Yeaman, filled with
colored men in chains, heading down the
Mississippi to the New Orleans slave markets.
It sickened me, 'n' more than that, it brought
a shadow down, a pall around my eyes.
(Beat.)
Slavery troubled me, as long as I can
remember, in a way it never troubled my
father, though he hated it. In his own fash-
ion. He knew no smallholding dirt farmer
could compete with slave plantations. He
took us out from Kentucky to get away
from 'em. He wanted Indiana kept free. He
wasn't a kind man, but there was a rough
moral urge for fairness, for freedom in
him. I learnt that from him, I suppose, if
little else from him. We didn't care for one
another, Mr. Yeaman.

GEORGE YEAMAN

(embarrassed:)
I . . . Well, I'm sorry to hear that—

LINCOLN

Loving-kindness, that most ordinary thing,
came to me from other sources. I'm grate-
ful for that.

GEORGE YEAMAN

I hate it, too, sir, slavery, but—but we're
entirely unready for emancipation. There's
too many questions—

LINCOLN

(laughs:)
We're unready for peace, too, ain't we?
When it comes, it'll present us with conun-

drums and dangers greater than any we've
faced during the war, bloody as it's been.
We'll have to extemporize and experiment
with *what* it is *when* it is.

Lincoln moves from the desk to take the seat beside Yeaman,
no longer towering over him. He leans forward and rests a
hand on Yeaman's knee.

> LINCOLN
> I read your speech, George. Negroes and
> the vote, that's a puzzle.

> GEORGE YEAMAN
> No, no, but, but, but—but Negroes can't,
> um, vote, Mr. Lincoln. You're not suggest-
> ing that we enfranchise colored people.

> LINCOLN
> I'm asking only that you disenthrall your-
> self from the slave powers. I'll let you know
> when there's an offer on my desk for sur-
> render.
> There's none before us now. What's before
> us now, that's the vote on the Thirteenth
> Amendment. It's going to be so very close.
> You see what you can do.

Lincoln leaves Yeaman, considering.

EXT. A WORKING-CLASS NEIGHBORHOOD IN
WASHINGTON—NIGHT

Lincoln stands in front of William Hutton's row house, talking to Hutton. The funeral wreath still hangs on the door
behind them, displaying the marks of time passing: faded,
weatherbeaten, dusty.

WILLIAM HUTTON

I can't make sense of it, what he died for.
Mr. Lincoln, I hate them all, I do, all black
people. I am a prejudiced man.

The door opens slightly behind Hutton. His wife looks out.
Hutton exchanges a glance with her, and the door shuts again.

LINCOLN

I'd change that in you if I could, but that's
not why I come. I might be wrong, Mr. Hutton, but I expect . . . Colored people will
most likely be free, and when that's so, it's
simple truth that your brother's bravery,
and his death, helped make it so. Only you
can decide whether that's sense enough for
you, or not.

Hutton walks slowly back to his house.

LINCOLN

My deepest sympathies to your family.

Lincoln goes back to his buggy. Hutton pauses at his door to
watch Lincoln's buggy drive away.

INT. LINCOLN'S OFFICE—NIGHT

Lincoln is seated at the head of the Cabinet table along with
Seward. Ashley, Preston and Monty Blair. Hay and Nicolay sit
in their usual chairs.

PRESTON BLAIR
(angry:)
We've managed our members to a fare-thee-
well, you've had no defections from the
Republican right to trouble you, whereas as

to what *you* promised— Where the hell are
the commissioners?!

JAMES ASHLEY

Oh God . . .
(to Lincoln:)
It's true! You, you . . . lied to me, Mr. Lincoln! You evaded my requests for a denial
that, that there is a Confederate peace offer
because, because there is one! We are abso-
lutely guaranteed to lose the whole thing—

JAMES ASHLEY	MONTGOMERY BLAIR
—and we'll be discredited, the amendment itself will be tainted. What if, what if these peace commissioners appear today? Or worse, on the morning—	We don't need a goddamned abolition amendment! Leave the Constitution alone! State by state you can extirpate—

LINCOLN

I can't listen to this anymore! I can't accomplish a goddamned thing of any human
meaning or worth until we cure ourselves of
slavery and end this pestilential war, and
whether any of you or anyone else knows
it, *I* know I need *this*! *This amendment is that
cure!* We're stepped out upon the world's
stage now, *now*, with the fate of human
dignity in our hands! Blood's been spilt to
afford us this moment!

He points around the table at Ashley, Monty, Preston.

LINCOLN

Now now now! And you grousle and heckle
and dodge about like pettifogging Tam-
many Hall hucksters! *See what is before you!
See the here and now!* That's the hardest

thing, the only thing that accounts! Abolishing slavery by constitutional provision settles the fate, for all coming time, not only of the millions now in bondage but of unborn millions to come. Two votes stand in its way, and these votes must be procured.

SEWARD

We need two yeses, three abstentions, or four yeses and one more abstention and the amendment will pass—

LINCOLN

You got a night and a day and a night and several perfectly good hours! Now get the hell out of here and get 'em!

JAMES ASHLEY

Yes but *how?*

LINCOLN

Buzzards' guts, man.

Lincoln rises, and keeps rising, till he seems eight feet tall.

LINCOLN

I am the President of the United States of America, *clothed in immense power!* You will procure me these votes.

INT. THE HOUSE CHAMBER—DAWN

The chamber is quiet and dark. PAGES and CLERKS prepare the desks, laying out pens and paper, filling inkwells.

TITLE:
THE MORNING OF THE VOTE
JANUARY 31, 1865

A CLERK is draping red-white-and-blue bunting on the desks of representatives from seceded states. These will of course remain unoccupied during the vote.

The first congressman to arrive, Thaddeus Stevens, clumps in. He goes to his desk and sits. He looks around the empty chamber, ready and waiting.

INT. THE HOUSE CHAMBER—MORNING, SEVERAL HOURS LATER

Thaddeus Stevens is at his desk. The House is in session, the floor full of congressmen caucusing and arguing.

The balcony's packed. Mary and Keckley sit at the front, Nicolay and Hay behind them. The Blairs are among other officials, rich people, foreign dignitaries.

There's a sudden quiet, then murmuring. Ashley, Stevens and everyone on the floor look up, Ellis, Hollister, Hutton and Hawkins among these.

In the balcony, twenty WELL-TO-DO BLACK PEOPLE, mostly men, are escorted by several senators, including Sumner and Wade, to a reserved section of the balcony. The black people glance at their surroundings but are rigidly composed.

Litton sees them enter. He looks about, at the representatives caucusing, or staring up at the visitors. Something powerful strikes him. In a voice coarse with emotion, he calls up to the black visitors:

> ASA VINTNER LITTON
> We welcome you, ladies and gentlemen,
> first in the history of this people's chamber,
> to *your House*!

There's tense applause. Some of the black guests bow; most aren't sure how to respond.

Yeaman watches this, deeply moved.

Bilbo catches Hawkins's eye and waves. Hawkins looks anxiously around, blushing.

Everyone is seated, and the place is packed.

Schuyler Colfax is in his high seat atop the rostrum, the SERGEANT-AT-ARMS to his right. Colfax gavels the House into session. Ashley is at the podium.

SCHUYLER COLFAX
Mr. Ashley, the floor is yours.

JAMES ASHLEY
On the matter of the joint resolution before us, presenting a Thirteenth Amendment to our national Constitution, which was passed last year by the Senate, and which has been debated now by this estimable body for the past several weeks. Today we will vote . . .

Cheers, boos, applause.

JAMES ASHLEY
By mutual agreement we shall hear *brief* final statements—

General cheering for this, laughing.

JAMES ASHLEY
—beginning with the honorable George Pendleton of Ohio.

Applause, boos. Pendleton, taking the podium, is handed several letters by Wood. He holds them over his head. The chamber's quiet.

GEORGE PENDLETON

I've just received confirmation of what previously has been merely rumored! *Affidavits*
from loyal citizens recently returned from
Richmond. They testify that commissioners
have indeed come North and ought to have
arrived by now in Washington City! Bearing
an offer of immediate cessation of our civil
war!

The chamber explodes. Through the ensuing ruckus:

FERNANDO WOOD

(to Ashley, fake shock:)
Are there Confederate commissioners in
the Capitol?

JAMES ASHLEY

I don't . . . I have no idea where they are or
if they've arrived or—

FERNANDO WOOD

If they've *arrived*?!

GEORGE PENDLETON

I appeal to my fellow Democrats, to all
Republican representatives who give a fig
for peace! Postpone this vote until we have
answers from the president himself!

In the balcony, Hay and Nicolay exchange worried glances.

FERNANDO WOOD

Postpone the vote!

Ashley turns to Stevens: "DO SOMETHING!" as Pendleton's
Democrats begin to chant: "POSTPONE THE VOTE!"

Mary, worried, looks from Mrs. Keckley to Preston Blair, who
is focused on the leader of the conservative Republican representatives, AARON HADDAM (R, KY). Haddam looks up
at Preston, awaiting instructions.

Democrats and Republicans rush to the Speaker to support
or protest the motion.

In the balcony, Preston slowly stands, saddened and angry.

> FERNANDO WOOD
> I have made a motion! Does anyone here
> care to second—

Preston nods at Haddam: "Go ahead." Haddam rises.

> AARON HADDAM
> (in a powerful voice:)
> Gentlemen.
> The conservative faction of border and
> western Republicans cannot approve this
> amendment, about which we harbor grave
> doubts, if a peace offer is being held hos-
> tage to its success. Joining with our Demo-
> cratic colleagues, I second the motion to
> postpone.

The debate swells again as, in the balcony, Schell scribbles
in a notebook while Latham whispers furiously in his ear.
Latham rips the page out before Schell's finished; Bilbo
snatches it from him.

> ROBERT LATHAM
> Quick, man! Quick!

Bilbo pushes his way out of the balcony. Nicolay, then Hay, follow on his heels. Mary sees this; she's concerned.

EXT. OUTSIDE THE CAPITOL—AFTERNOON

Hay and Nicolay emerge. They see Bilbo running, far ahead. Hay immediately sprints after him and trips. Nicolay continues running.

INT/EXT. WHITE HOUSE PORTICO, FOYER, STAIRS—AFTERNOON

Bilbo puffs his way across the portico, through the door, and up the stairs. Hay gains on him. It's become a race!

In the second floor hallway, Bilbo gets winded, and Hay dashes past him. Hay reaches the doors to Lincoln's office and flings them open.

INT. LINCOLN'S OFFICE, THE WHITE HOUSE—AFTERNOON

Lincoln is at his desk, working, when Hay bursts in. Bilbo appears in the doorway, beet-red and gasping for air.

Hay's too winded to speak. Bilbo holds out the note, limp with sweat, and brings it to Lincoln. Lincoln reads it.

> LINCOLN
> This is precisely what Mr. Wood wishes me
> to respond to?

Tad runs into the room, excited by the commotion. He wraps his arms around his father's neck, then tears wildly out of the room.

LINCOLN

Word for word? This is precisely the assur-
ance that he demands of me?

W. N. BILBO

Yes, sir.

As Nicolay heaves into the room in last place, wheezing ter-
ribly, Lincoln deliberates for a moment, then writes a note.
He blots, folds and hands it to Hay, who immediately reads
it, Nicolay looking on.

LINCOLN

Give this to Mr. Ashley.

Hay looks at Nicolay, who can't speak; he waves at Hay to
speak for him.

JOHN HAY

I feel, um, I have to say, Mr. Lincoln, that
this—
            (annoyed, impatient, to Bilbo:)
Could you please just step outside?!

W. N. BILBO

You gonna have a chat now, with the whole
of the House of Representatives waiting on
that?

Nicolay continues gasping, trying to speak. He can't.

JOHN HAY

            (to Lincoln:)
Making false representation to Congress is,
it's, um—

JOHN NICOLAY

It's, it's—

LINCOLN
Impeachable. I've made no false representation.

JOHN HAY
But there *are*—
(whispering:)
There *is* a delegation from Richmond.

LINCOLN
Give me the note, Johnnie.

Hay gives Lincoln the note. Lincoln takes it, holding on to
Hay's hand; with his free hand, Lincoln passes the note to
Bilbo.

LINCOLN
(to Bilbo:)
Please deliver that to Mr. Ashley.

INT. THE HOUSE CHAMBER AND BALCONY—
AFTERNOON

Bilbo, pushing past the pages, runs in, holding the note;
Ashley snatches it, reading as he makes his way to the
podium. All eyes are on Ashley.

JAMES ASHLEY
From the president:

The chamber falls silent.

JAMES ASHLEY
"So far as I know, there are no peace commissioners in the city nor are there likely to be."

Applause, booing, furious discussion.

GEORGE PENDLETON
"So far as I know—"?! That means nothing!
Are there commissioners from the South or
aren't there?!

In the balcony, Mary looks to Mrs. Keckley.

JAMES ASHLEY
The president has answered you, sir! Your
peace offer is a fiction!

GEORGE PENDLETON
That is not a *denial*, it is a lawyer's dodge!

JAMES ASHLEY
Mr. Haddam? Is your faction satisfied?

Preston, in the balcony, hesitates. He looks at his daughter, who
gives him a questioning look: "Do you want this on your head?"

He doesn't. He indicates to Haddam with a small shake of
his venerable head: "Drop it."

AARON HADDAM
The conservative Republican faction's satisfied, and we thank Mr. Lincoln. I move to
table Mr. Wood's motion.

SCHUYLER COLFAX
Tabled!

There's an angry response, but Wood and Pendleton sit,
thwarted.

JAMES ASHLEY
Speaker Colfax, I order the main question.

SCHUYLER COLFAX
A motion has been made to bring the bill
for the Thirteenth Amendment to a vote.
Do I hear a second?

ASA VINTNER LITTON
I second the motion.

SCHUYLER COLFAX
So moved, so ordered. The clerk will now—
        (a rap of the gavel:)
Quiet please.

The noise of the chamber and balcony reduce to a rumble.

SCHUYLER COLFAX
The clerk will now call the roll for voting.

Thaddeus Stevens sits silently, tired, concentrated: the
moment has come.

THE CLERK OF THE HOUSE
We begin with Connecticut. Mr. Augustus
Benjamin, on the matter of this amend-
ment, how say you?

The chamber is completely silent for the first time.

AUGUSTUS BENJAMIN
Nay!

The Clerk records his vote.

THE CLERK OF THE HOUSE
Mr. Arthur Bentleigh.

ARTHUR BENTLEIGH
Nay!

THE CLERK OF THE HOUSE
Mr. John Ellis, how say you?

JOHN ELLIS
Aye!

Angry shouts from Ellis's fellow Democrats, forcing Colfax
to gavel for order.

DEMOCRATIC SENATOR
What?! Shameful!

THE CLERK OF THE HOUSE
Missouri next. Mr. Walter Appleton.

WALTER APPLETON
I vote no!

THE CLERK OF THE HOUSE
Mr. Josiah Burton.

JOSIAH BURTON rises to his feet. He is very, very tall and thin.

JOSIAH BURTON
Beanpole Burton is pleased to vote yea!

Mary watches from the balcony, pleased, but anxious.

THE CLERK OF THE HOUSE
The State of New Jersey. Mr. Nehemiah
Cleary.

NEHEMIAH CLEARY
No.

THE CLERK OF THE HOUSE
Mr. James Martinson.

JAMES ASHLEY
Mr. Martinson has delegated me to say he is
indisposed and he abstains.

THE CLERK OF THE HOUSE
Mr. Austin J. Roberts.

JAMES ASHLEY
Also indisposed, also abstaining.

Shocked anger from the Democrats. Pendleton starts calcu-
lating votes on a sheet of paper. Wood grabs it and begins to
calculate more rapidly.

In the balcony, Mary keeps track on her own list. She writes
carefully next to Roberts's name: "15 TO WIN"

THE CLERK OF THE HOUSE
Illinois concluded. Mr. Harold Hollister,
how say you?

Hollister glowers next to Hutton, who's silently praying.

HAROLD HOLLISTER
No.

THE CLERK OF THE HOUSE
Mr. Hutton? Mr. William Hutton, cast your
vote.

Hutton looks up from his prayer.

WILLIAM HUTTON
William Hutton, remembering at this
moment his beloved brother, Frederick,
votes against the amendment.

INT. LINCOLN'S OFFICE, THE WHITE HOUSE—
AFTERNOON

Lincoln watches Tad stacking books to make a fort for his
lead toy soldiers.

INT./EXT. ROTUNDA AND FRONT DOOR OF THE
CAPITOL—AFTERNOON

A field telegraph has been set up near the steps, at the front
of the enormous crowd that's assembled before the Capitol.
Poles are held up in the crowd by SOLDIERS along which
the telegraph wire is stretched.

A SOLDIER stationed at the door of the Capitol relays the
vote to ANOTHER SOLDIER manning the cipher key:

> SOLDIER
> Webster Allen votes no.

The cipher operator instantly transmits.

INT. GRANT'S TELEGRAPH ROOM AT CITY POINT—
AFTERNOON

OFFICERS are crowded in the small room, watching a SER-
GEANT transcribe as his cipher key clicks.

> SERGEANT
> Webster Allen, Illinois, Democrat, votes . . .
> no.

The cipher key clicks again.

> SERGEANT
> Halberd Law, Indiana, Democrat, votes . . .
> no.

Grant observes this from the balcony above. Robert, in a captain's uniform, stands near him. Like his mother, Robert has a scorecard, and he's keeping track.

Grant turns his back on the proceedings to light a cigar. He's concerned at how close the vote is. Behind him the count continues:

> SERGEANT
> Archibald Moran . . . yes.

Robert has been looking at Grant; he returns to his score keeping.

> SERGEANT
> Ambrose Bailer . . . yes.

INT. THE HOUSE CHAMBER AND BALCONY—
AFTERNOON

The Clerk continues.

> THE CLERK OF THE HOUSE
> Mr. Walter H. Washburn.

> WALTER H. WASHBURN
> Votes no.

> THE CLERK OF THE HOUSE
> And Mr. George Yeaman, how say you?

Yeaman doesn't respond. The silence this causes lengthens, till representatives begin to look to see what's happened. Yeaman sits, staring ahead, not responding. Thaddeus Stevens, sensing something's happening, looks in Yeaman's direction. Yeaman, still staring ahead, mumbles something, but it's inaudible.

THE CLERK OF THE HOUSE
Sorry Mr. Yeaman, I didn't hear you vote—

GEORGE YEAMAN
(rising to his feet:)
I said aye, Mr. McPherson.
AYE!!!

Great surprise, loud cheers and angry shouts.

FERNANDO WOOD
TRAITOR! TRAITOR!

Yeaman looks ready to faint. To the consternation of the Democrats, a mob of gleeful Republicans rushes across the aisle that separates the two parties; they surround Yeaman, shaking his hand, slapping him on the back. Colfax bangs the gavel.

SCHUYLER COLFAX
Order!

Pendleton is speechless. Litton turns to Ashley, both astonished; Ashley turns to Stevens, who watches, sharp, observant, giving nothing away.

Mary updates her tally: "8 TO WIN"

SCHUYLER COLFAX
Order in the chamber!

Yeaman collapses back into his seat. The room quiets.

SCHUYLER COLFAX
Mr. McPherson, you may proceed.

THE CLERK OF THE HOUSE
Mr. Clay R. Hawkins of Ohio.

Hawkins seems to have been startled out of a reverie. Sick
with fear, he looks up at the sound of his name. He can't
speak. Wood and Pendleton watch this, deeply alarmed.
Hawkins snaps out of it.

CLAY HAWKINS
Goddamn it, I'm voting yes.

A huge reaction to this. LeClerk gapes at Hawkins.

CLAY HAWKINS
(right at Pendleton and Wood:)
I don't care, shoot me dead! You shoot me
dead I, I am voting yes!

THE CLERK OF THE HOUSE
Mr. Edwin F. LeClerk.

LeClerk, seated next to Hawkins and transfixed by his courage, turns dazedly to McPherson.

EDWIN LECLERK
No.
(then, standing abruptly:)
Oh to hell with it, shoot me dead, too. Yes!

The noise gets wilder. Pendleton fixes LeClerk and Hawkins
with a murderous look.

EDWIN LECLERK
I mean, abstention. Abstention.

Disgust briefly flashing across his face, McPherson crosses
out and changes LeClerk's vote to an abstention. The cheering and booing degenerates to intense argument about what
this means for the vote count.

In the balcony, Bilbo looks at Hawkins, well-pleased.

THE CLERK OF THE HOUSE
Mr. Alexander Coffroth.

Coffroth looks toward Stevens, who doesn't look at him.

ALEXANDER COFFROTH
(proud of himself and happy about the
reward he'll get:)
I. Vote. Yes.

Applause. Stevens still doesn't look at Coffroth, but, tickled,
he grins and nods.

INT. GRANT'S TELEGRAPH ROOM AT CITY POINT—
AFTERNOON

Grant stands with Robert at the balcony rail, waiting.

SERGEANT
James Brooks . . . nay.

On a nearby board, a large map has been tacked back-
ward; on its reverse side, the count is being scrawled by an
OFFICER, who marks off the votes in quintiles in columns
marked "yea" and "nay."

SERGEANT
Josiah Grinnell . . . yea. Meyer Straus . . .

INT. THE HOUSE CHAMBER AND BALCONY—
AFTERNOON

STRAUS rises.

MEYER STRAUS
Nay.

THE CLERK OF THE HOUSE
Mr. Joseph Marstern?

JOSEPH MARSTERN
Nay.

THE CLERK OF THE HOUSE
Mr. Chilton A. Elliot?

CHILTON A. ELLIOT
No!

THE CLERK OF THE HOUSE
Mr. Daniel G. Stuart?

DANIEL G. STUART
I vote yes.

Then, in a sequence of rapid cuts:

THE CLERK OF THE HOUSE
Mr. Howard Guilefoyle.

HOWARD GUILEFOYLE
Yea.

THE CLERK OF THE HOUSE
John F. McKenzie.

JOHN F. MCKENZIE
Yea.

THE CLERK OF THE HOUSE
Andrew E. Fink.

ANDREW E. FINK
Nay.

> THE CLERK OF THE HOUSE
> Mr. John A. Kassim.

> JOHN A. KASSIM
> Yea.

> THE CLERK OF THE HOUSE
> Mr. Hanready.

> AVON HANREADY
> Nay.

> THE CLERK OF THE HOUSE
> And Mr. Rufus Warren?

> RUFUS WARREN
> Yea.

INT. LINCOLN'S OFFICE, THE WHITE HOUSE—
AFTERNOON

Tad is on Lincoln's lap. They're examining a book, the
pages of which feature illustrations comparing the varieties
of species of insects, zebras, finches.

INT. THE HOUSE CHAMBER AND BALCONY—
AFTERNOON

The room is quiet and tense.

> THE CLERK OF THE HOUSE
> The roll call concludes, voting is completed,
> now—

> SCHUYLER COLFAX
> Mr. Clerk, please call my name, I want to
> cast a vote.

GEORGE PENDLETON
I object! The Speaker doesn't vote!

SCHUYLER COLFAX
The Speaker *may* vote if he so chooses.

GEORGE PENDLETON
It is highly unusual, sir—

SCHUYLER COLFAX
This isn't usual, Mr. Pendleton, this is history.

THE CLERK OF THE HOUSE
How does Mr. Schuyler Colfax vote?

SCHUYLER COLFAX
(a look of surprise that this needs to be
asked, then, stating the obvious:)
Aye, of course.

Laughter in the chamber. The Clerk tallies the vote, then passes the recorded vote to the Speaker. There's absolute silence.

In the balcony, Mary checks her own tally, not quite believing it.

SCHUYLER COLFAX
The final vote: 8 absent or not voting, 56
votes against, 119 votes for. With a margin
of 2 votes—

INT. LINCOLN'S OFFICE, THE WHITE HOUSE—
AFTERNOON

Lincoln stands, waiting. The only sound is the ticking of the clock. And then the ticking is slowly drowned out as bells begin to peal throughout the city. Lincoln raises the window as Tad rushes to him. The bells are joined by a cannonade. The sound of jubilation fills his office.

Lincoln turns from the window to Tad, who stares out eagerly, seeking out the source of the noise. Lincoln puts his hand on Tad's head. He looks down at his son, silent.

INT. THE HOUSE CHAMBER, THE CAPITOL—LATE AFTERNOON

Representatives throw papers in the air, embrace, weep, shout, dance, climb on desks. In the balcony, Mary stands slowly, beyond tears or joy; Mrs. Keckley stands with her, smiling, crying. Preston Blair applauds vigorously. The black visitors join the general exultation, overwhelmed, some praying, others embracing and weeping.

Latham, Schell and Bilbo's seats are empty; they've gone.

Ashley, grinning from ear to ear, tears streaming down his face, is hoisted up on shoulders and marched around the room, as on the floor and in the balcony, people start singing "The Battle Cry of Freedom."

Pendleton, with the face of someone who's seen his world collapse into ruin, walks straight at Yeaman, who's listening to the singing, deeply moved, his face full of wonder. Pendleton turns, without a word, and leaves the House.

Yeaman laughs, and loudly joins in singing.

Stevens clumps over to the Clerk, who is placing his tallies and the official copy of the amendment bill in a folio. He looks up.

THE CLERK OF THE HOUSE
Congratulations, Mr. Chairman.

> THADDEUS STEVENS
> The bill, Mr. McPherson, may I . . . ?

The Clerk hands the bill to Stevens, who folds it and pockets it.

> THE CLERK OF THE HOUSE
> That's . . . That's the official bill.

> THADDEUS STEVENS
> I'll return it in the morning. Creased, but
> unharmed.

EXT. A STREET, WASHINGTON—DUSK

Celebrating crowds move toward the Mall, singing, carrying placards proclaiming the passage of the amendment.

Thaddeus Stevens is hobbling in the opposite direction, making difficult headway against the crowd, pushed and shoved, unrecognized; he shoves back, his ferocious scowl utterly at odds with the prevailing festive mood.

He reaches a modest house, unlocks the door and steps inside.

INT. THADDEUS STEVENS'S HOUSE—NIGHT

Stevens is met at the door by LYDIA SMITH, a black woman in her fifties. As she helps him off with his coat, he takes a piece of paper from his pocket.

> THADDEUS STEVENS
> A gift for you.

She takes it.

THADDEUS STEVENS
The greatest measure of the nineteenth
century. Passed by corruption, aided and
abetted by the purest man in America.

INT. THE BEDROOM IN THADDEUS STEVENS'S
HOUSE—NIGHT

Stevens, in his nightgown, takes off his wig. He's bald.

He lies down in bed. Lydia Smith is in bed already beside
him. She's holding the paper he gave her.

THADDEUS STEVENS
I wish you'd been present.

LYDIA SMITH
I wish I'd been.

THADDEUS STEVENS
It was a spectacle.

LYDIA SMITH
You can't bring your housekeeper to the
House. I won't give them gossip.
    (the paper:)
This is enough. This is . . . It's more than
enough for now.

They kiss. He lies back. He grabs her hand.

THADDEUS STEVENS
Read it to me again, my love.

LYDIA SMITH
"Proposed—"

THADDEUS STEVENS
And adopted.

LYDIA SMITH
Adopted. "An Amendment to the Constitution of the United States. Section One:
Neither slavery nor involuntary servitude,
except as a punishment for crime whereof
the party shall have been duly convicted,
shall exist within the United States, or any
place subject to their jurisdiction."

THADDEUS STEVENS
Section Two:

LYDIA SMITH
"Congress shall have power to enforce this
amendment by appropriate legislation."

Thaddeus Stevens grins, nods, thinking, eyes sparkling.

INT./EXT. THE DOCK AT FORTRESS MONROE,
HAMPTON ROADS, VIRGINIA—LATE AFTERNOON

Sailors cheer Lincoln's arrival. Lincoln walks across the
gangway. Seward greets him amidst the cheers.

INT. THE SALOON ON BOARD THE RIVER QUEEN,
HAMPTON ROADS, VIRGINIA—DAY

Lincoln and Seward are at a table facing the three Confederate peace commissioners. Seward looks concerned at Lincoln's fatigue.

ALEXANDER STEPHENS
Let me be blunt. Will the Southern states
resume their former position in the Union

speedily enough to enable us to block ratifi-
cation of the Thirteenth Amendment?

LINCOLN
I'd like peace immediately.

ALEXANDER STEPHENS
Yes, and . . . ?

LINCOLN
I'd like your states restored to their practi-
cal relations to the Union immediately.

Silence.

ALEXANDER STEPHENS
If this could be given me in writing, as Vice
President of the Confederacy, I'd bring that
document with celerity to Jefferson Davis.

SEWARD
Surrender and we can discuss reconstruction.

ALEXANDER STEPHENS
Surrender won't be thought of unless you've
assured us, in writing, that we'll be readmitted in time to block this amendment.

R. M. T. HUNTER
This is the arrogant demand of a conqueror
for a humiliating, abject—

SEWARD
You'll not be conquered people, Mr.
Hunter. You will be citizens, returned to
the laws and the guarantees of rights of the
Constitution.

ALEXANDER STEPHENS
Which now extinguishes slavery. And with
it our economy. All our laws will be deter-
mined by a Congress of vengeful Yankees,
all our rights'll be subject to a Supreme
Court benched by black Republican radicals. All our traditions will be obliterated.
We won't know ourselves anymore.

LINCOLN
(a nod, then:)
We ain't here to discuss reconstruction, we
have no legal basis for that discussion. But
I don't want to deal falsely. The Northern
states'll ratify, most of 'em. As I figure, it
remains for two of the Southern states to do
the same, even after all are readmitted. And
I been working on that.

ALEXANDER STEPHENS
Tennessee and Louisiana.

LINCOLN
Arkansas, too, most likely. It'll be ratified.
Slavery, sir, it's done.

Hunter storms out of the cabin.

LINCOLN
If we submit ourselves to law, Alex, even
submit to losing freedoms—the freedom
to oppress, for instance—we may discover
other freedoms previously unknown to us.
Had you kept faith with democratic process,
as frustrating as that can be—

JOHN A. CAMPBELL
Come, sir, spare us at least these pieties. Did
you defeat us with ballots?

ALEXANDER STEPHENS
How've you held your Union together?
Through *democracy*? How many hundreds of
thousands have died during your administration? Your Union, sir, is bonded in can-
nonfire and death.

LINCOLN
It may be you're right. But say all we done is
show the world that democracy isn't chaos,
that there is a great invisible strength in
a people's union? Say we've shown that a
people can endure awful sacrifice and yet
cohere? Mightn't that save at least the *idea*
of democracy, to aspire to? Eventually, to
become worthy of? At all rates, whatever
may be proven by blood and sacrifice
must've been proved by now. Shall we stop
this bleeding?

EXT. A CITY ON A SOUTHERN RIVER—NIGHT

Like a vision of apocalypse, a city on the banks of a broad
river is being consumed in a hellish fire, as artillery shells
rend the dark sky asunder, raining down destruction.

EXT. SIEGE LINES BEFORE PETERSBURG, VIRGINIA—
MORNING

The morning is gray, and a dense fog covers a vast field.
Lincoln, his stovepipe hat atop his head, is mounted on a
horse on a rise at one end of the field. Behind him, several
UNION OFFICERS are also mounted. It's chilly; the breath
of the men and the horses is visible.

TITLE:
OUTSIDE PETERSBURG, VIRGINIA
APRIL 3

Lincoln flicks the reins of his horse, which starts down the slope. The officers follow behind him. No one speaks.

Lincoln rides slowly, his focus on the ground before him. Debris is scattered all around him, along with the bodies of fallen soldiers.

He looks up and across the battlefield; a terrible battle has concluded a couple of hours ago.

Looking down, as he rides, he sees soldiers killed by artillery fire, whose bodies lie twisted, burned, headless, limbless, torn in two, blown out of their clothing or charred too badly to tell. He sees soldiers killed by rifle and bayonet, whose corpses are intact.

At the beginning of his ride, all the dead and wounded are in Union blue, the casualties of Confederate cannon fire, felled as the Union Army, about six hours earlier, began its final, successful drive to break through Confederate lines.

As Lincoln and his escorts move across the battlefield, gray-and-blue uniformed corpses and badly wounded men intermingle.

He reaches the other side of the field, passing a Confederate flag to enter the now-ruined town of Petersburg.

EXT. THE THOMAS WALLACE HOUSE, GRANT'S
TEMPORARY HEADQUARTERS, ON MARKET STREET,
PETERSBURG—MORNING

Grant, smoking his cigar, his uniform dusty and rumpled, is sitting on the small porch. He stares piercingly at Lincoln, in

a rocker next to him, watching his troops pass by as they move
in to secure the conquered town. Lincoln closes his eyes.

He has grown older, the skin around his eyes is cobwebbed
with fine creases, and his hair's thinner, softer, suffused with
gray. His brow has grown smoother.

LINCOLN
Once he surrenders, send his boys back to
their homes, their farms, their shops.

GRANT
Yes, sir, as we discussed.

LINCOLN
Liberality all around. No punishment.
I don't want that. And the leaders—Jeff
and the rest of 'em—if they escape, leave
the country while my back's turned, that
wouldn't upset me none.
When peace comes it mustn't just be hangings.

GRANT
By outward appearance, you're ten years
older than you were a year ago.

LINCOLN
Some weariness has bit at my bones.
　(Beat.)
I never seen the like of it before. What
I seen today. Never seen the like of it before.

GRANT
You always knew that, what this was going to
be. Intimate, and ugly.
You must've needed to see it close when you
decided to come down here.

LINCOLN
We've made it possible for one another to
do terrible things.

GRANT
And we've won the war. Now you have to
lead us out of it.

EXT. THE MCLEAN HOUSE, APPOMATTOX COURT
HOUSE, VIRGINIA—AFTERNOON

CONFEDERATE and UNION OFFICERS stand around
in the afternoon sun. Everyone's solemn, even stunned by
what's just happened. No one is speaking.

TITLE:
APPOMATTOX COURTHOUSE, VIRGINIA
APRIL 9, 1865

ROBERT E. LEE comes down the steps of the McLean
house, as a CONFEDERATE OFFICER brings his horse to
him. His face is blank. Lee mounts his waiting horse.

Lee should leave, having just surrendered to Grant inside;
but he's immobile. Some of the officers of both sides look
at Lee, some can't bear it. Lee tries out various expressions:
pride, defiance, blankness.

Grant stomps onto the porch of the house, followed by his
staff. Among them is Robert Lincoln.

Grant, lost in thought, stops, taken aback, realizing that
Lee's still there, astride his horse. Everyone looks at the two
men who look awkwardly at one another.

Then Grant removes his famous slouch hat. Everyone
freezes for a moment, and then one by one, the officers of
the Union Army remove their hats.

Lee is visibly moved by this gesture of respect. He raises his hat, briefly, only an inch from his head. Then, pulling slightly on his horse's reins, he rides away.

EXT. A BUGGY RIDE THROUGH WASHINGTON—
AFTERNOON

A beautiful spring afternoon. Lincoln and Mary are riding in the buggy, driven by the old soldier.

MARY
You've an itch to travel?

LINCOLN
I'd like that. To the West by rail.

MARY
(shaking her head no:)
Overseas.

LINCOLN
The Holy Land.

MARY
(a laugh, then:)
Awfully pious for a man who takes his wife
out buggy-riding on Good Friday.

LINCOLN
Jerusalem. Where David and Solomon
walked. I dream of walking in that ancient
city.

She seems sadder. They ride in silence.

MARY
All anyone will remember of me is I was
crazy and I ruined your happiness.

LINCOLN
Anyone thinks that doesn't understand,
Molly.

She nods; then, tenderly:

MARY
When they look at you, at what it cost to
live at the heart of this, they'll wonder at
it. They'll wonder at you. They should.
But they should also look at the wretched
woman by your side, if they want to understand what this was truly like. For an ordinary person. For anyone other than you.

Lincoln laughs, takes her hand. She leans against him.

LINCOLN
We must try to be happier. We must. Both
of us. We've been so miserable for so long.

INT. LINCOLN'S OFFICE—EVENING

Lincoln's in the shirtsleeves and vest of his formal evening
wear, his hair brushed down and plastered in place. William
Slade is working the tie and gloves. James Ashley and Schuyler Colfax stand with Lincoln, holding glasses of scotch
whiskey. Slade waits with Lincoln's coat, clothes brush, the
stovepipe hat and gloves on the table.

John Hay tears down several of the military maps, heavily
marked, from the bookcases where they're tacked. He drops
these on the floor. As they watch Hay:

LINCOLN
I did say *some* colored men, the intelligent,
the educated, and veterans, I qualified it.

JAMES ASHLEY
Mr. Stevens is furious, he wants to know why
you qualified it—

SCHUYLER COLFAX
No one heard the intelligent or the educated part. All they heard was the first time
any president has ever made mention of
Negro voting.

LINCOLN
Still, I wish I'd mentioned it in a better
speech.

JAMES ASHLEY
Mr. Stevens also wants to know why you
didn't make a better speech.

They laugh. There's a knock on the door; Nicolay enters.

JOHN NICOLAY
(to Lincoln:)
Mrs. Lincoln's waiting in the carriage. She
wants me to remind you of the hour, and
that you'll have to pick up Miss Harris and
Major Rathbone.

Lincoln nods. Slade enters with Lincoln's hat, coat and
gloves. Lincoln begins to dress hurriedly.

LINCOLN
Am I in trouble?

WILLIAM SLADE
No, sir.

LINCOLN
Thank you, Mr. Slade.

Slade hands Lincoln his gloves as Colfax and Ashley drain
their drinks and rise.

                    LINCOLN
          I suppose it's time to go, though I would
          rather stay.

Tossing his gloves on a side table as he goes, Lincoln leaves
the room.

INT. AN EMPTY CORRIDOR, SECOND FLOOR OF THE
WHITE HOUSE—CONTINUOUS

Lincoln walks past the petitioners chairs. Slade enters the
hallway from the office with the discarded gloves, in pursuit.
Then Slade stops, thinking better of it. He's walking back
toward the office when, arrested by a strange feeling, he
turns around again. Slade watches Lincoln walk down the
empty corridor, until he's gone.

INT. A THEATER—NIGHT

The theater is adorned with patriotic bunting.

Onstage, a caliph's palace. A YOUNG MAN duels with scimi-
tars against a huge, hideous AFRIT. A YOUNG WOMAN
in chains cowers in distress. The young man gymnastically
avoids being killed, then plunges his scimitar into the afrit's
heart. The demon screams and topples to the ground. The
audience gasps as a flame-colored, bejeweled bird rises up
from the dead afrit's heart.

The audience applauds. In the center box, Tad Lincoln is
joining in, as is his companion for the evening, Tom Pendel.

Onstage, the bird flies off, the young man is freeing the
young woman, when the scene is halted by the red curtain
lowering, surprising actors and audience. The music dies, the
gas lights in the house are being raised as the owner of the
theater, LEONARD GROVER, steps out before the curtain
and walks to the center of the stage, pale and badly shaken.

In the box, Tom Pendel glances quickly at Tad, who's fixed
on the stage, eyes open, alarmed.

The audience knows something's wrong. Their rising murmur
of concern dies immediately when Grover raises his hands.

LEONARD GROVER
(voice shaking:)
The president has been shot.

There are screams of horror from the audience; people leap
from their seats.

LEONARD GROVER
The president has been shot at Ford's Theatre!

The theater is a scene of complete pandemonium. People
cry, jam the aisles, call to each other across rows of seats,
shout questions at Grover, who's calling for calm, inaudible
in the uproar.

Tom Pendel is frozen in shock, then turns to draw Tad close
to him. Tad pulls away and begins shrieking, clinging to the
railing so tightly that Pendel can't pry him loose. Tad can't
stop screaming, his eyes wide open, seeing nothing.

INT. THE BEDROOM IN PETERSON'S BOARDING
HOUSE—MORNING

Mary is gently escorted into a tiny room. A small, hissing gas
jet in the wall bathes the scene with green light.

Stanton, Speed, GENERAL HENRY HALLECK and a MINISTER, are standing. Welles sits by the head of the bed. DR. CHARLES LEALE, a young army surgeon, and DR. ROBERT STONE, the Lincoln family's doctor, stand uselessly by the foot of the bed, while DR. JOSEPH BARNES, the Surgeon General, listens to Lincoln's faint breathing.

Robert, in uniform, red-eyed, pale as a ghost, sits at the bedside and stares at his father, barely breathing.

Lincoln lies in a crooked diagonal, his knees bent, on a bed he's too tall to fit properly, clad only in a nightshirt.

Barnes moves his head closer, then closer. The room is utterly still. Barnes takes out his watch, looks at the time, softly clears his throat.

> DR. BARNES
> It's 7:22 in the morning, Saturday the 15th
> of April. It's all over. The president is no
> more.

No one talks, or moves.

Stanton looks at Lincoln's body.

> STANTON
> Now he belongs to the ages.

Robert begins to weep.

> LINCOLN (V.O.)
> Fondly do we hope, fervently do we pray,
> that this mighty scourge of war may speedily
> pass away.

EXT. THE EAST PORTICO OF THE CAPITOL—NOON

Lincoln, wearing spectacles, stands at a podium before the
Capitol dome, still under scaffolding, under cloudy skies. He
reads from the two pages.

> LINCOLN
> Yet, if God wills that it continue until all the
> wealth piled by the bondman's two hundred
> and fifty years of unrequited toil shall be
> sunk, and until every drop of blood drawn
> with the lash shall be paid by another drawn
> with the sword, as was said three thousand
> years ago, so still it must be said "the judg-
> ments of the Lord are true and righteous
> altogether."

He glances at his audience: forty thousand people from all
over the country, wounded soldiers, civilians in black. And
for the first time, *in* the crowd, not at its edges, hundreds of
African Americans, civilians and soldiers.

> LINCOLN
> With malice toward none, with charity for
> all, with firmness in the right as God gives
> us to see the right, let us strive on to finish
> the work we are in, to bind up the nation's
> wounds, to care for him who shall have
> borne the battle, and for his widow and his
> orphan, to do all which may achieve and
> cherish a just and a lasting peace among
> ourselves and with all nations.

FADE TO BLACK

THE END

ACKNOWLEDGMENTS

In my work on the screenplay for *Lincoln* I incurred many debts. Though by no means complete, the list that follows includes those people without whose collaboration, scholarly work and/or emotional and intellectual support, the script would not have been written, and/or the screenwriter wouldn't have made it through intact (more or less): Samantha Becker, Gabor S. Borritt, Michael Burlingame, Daniel Day-Lewis, Oskar Eustis, Drew Gilpin Faust, Doris Kearns Goodwin, Antonia Grilikhes-Lasky, Allen Guelzo, Mark Harris, Harold Holzer, Kathy Kennedy, Joyce Ketay, Kristie Macosko Krieger, Eric Kushner, Lesley Kushner, William Kushner, James M. McPherson, Andrew Russell, Frank Selvaggi, Maurice Sendak, Brian J. Siberell, Tommy Sobel, Adam Somner, Ian Stone, Jeanine Tesori, Kyle Warren and, above all, Steven Spielberg.

Tony Kushner's plays include *A Bright Room Called Day*; *Angels in America, Parts One and Two*; *Slavs!*; *Homebody/Kabul*; the musical *Caroline, or Change* and the opera *A Blizzard on Marblehead Neck*, both with composer Jeanine Tesori; and *The Intelligent Homosexual's Guide to Capitalism and Socialism with a Key to the Scriptures*. He has adapted and translated Pierre Corneille's *The Illusion*, S. Y. Ansky's *The Dybbuk*, Bertolt Brecht's *The Good Person of Szechuan* and *Mother Courage and Her Children*; and the English-language libretto for the opera *Brundibár* by Hans Krása. He wrote the screenplays for Mike Nichols's film of *Angels in America*, and for Steven Spielberg's *Munich*. His books include *Brundibar*, with illustrations by Maurice Sendak; *The Art of Maurice Sendak, 1980 to the Present*; and *Wrestling with Zion: Progressive Jewish-American Responses to the Palestinian/Israeli Conflict*, co-edited with Alisa Solomon. Kushner is the recipient of a Pulitzer Prize, two Tony Awards, three Obie Awards, two Evening Standard Awards, an Olivier Award, an Emmy Award and an Oscar nomination, and the Steinberg Distinguished Playwright Award, among other honors. He lives in Manhattan with his husband Mark Harris.